Self-Care:

A Better Version of Me

How to Avoid Burnout, Refocus your Attention, Reclaim your Time, and Become a Better Version of You

By LaToya D. Thomas

Preface

This personal development self-help book has two purposes: to share my personal self-care journey and to help other people who are also on a self-care journey or may need to start one. My goal is to inspire and motivate readers to become the best versions of themselves, one step at a time.

My story began more than a decade ago and continues today. As I share my story, I also offer advice and ideas related to self-care. You'll read the stories of Ciara, Lisa, and Shawn. Then, you'll finish with the rest of my personal story, including how I overcame much of what I experienced and how I began to live in my purpose, ultimately becoming a better version of myself.

Knowing that life takes us on twists and turns, similar to a rollercoaster ride, and can be extremely unpredictable makes the journey one heck of a ride. Know that you are not alone, even if, at times, it feels that way. Let the pages in this book guide and comfort you, motivate and inspire you, and if you know someone else who may resonate with the message, please share it with them. You could be the reason they begin to focus on themselves unselfishly.

Follow your joy,

LaToya D. Thomas

Dedication

The world is a better place with caring people in it. I want to take a moment to thank a few of the most caring people I know. You all played a critical role in the development of this book and my self-care journey, even if you didn't know it at the time. Thank you for being amazing human beings.

Anna Lall

Brian Lall

Charissa Myers, MD

Jadyn Thomas-Leslie

Mary Carlyle

To my kiddos, Jadyn, Jacques, and Miani - Thank you for your patience when I needed time to write. I know it was not easy. I hope I've inspired you to follow your dreams, live in your purpose, and shine your lights in the lives of others.

Contents

Preface iii

Dedication iv

Introduction 1

Chapter 1 10

Burnout: Pouring from an Empty Cup 10

What is burnout? 17

What causes burnout? 18

Symptoms of Burnout/Untreated Burnout 19

Key Takeaways 20

Notes 24

Chapter 2 27

Identifying Barriers 27

When your barrier is a limiting belief system or lack of resources 28

When your barrier is a person or group of people 32

People-Pleasing 32

Social Expectations 33

Toxic Associations & Unhealthy Relationships 34

When Your Barrier is You 38

Other Types of Barriers 46

Key Takeaways 57

Chapter 3 61

Self-Discovery 61

Self-Discovery 62

Self-Awareness 63

Self-Discovery and Self-Awareness 65

Key Takeaways...71

Chapter 4 75

Ciara...75

Small Changes that Could Positively Affect Ciara.........83

Chapter 5 90

The Myths of Self-care 90

Key Takeaways..101

Chapter 6 104

The Breakthrough..104

Chapter 7 112

Adopting a...112

"Me-First" Mentality 112

Why Saying "No" is Important..................................116

How to Say "No" 117

Establishing New Habits 120

Key Takeaways..122

Chapter 8 125

What can Self-care Look Like?.................................125

Key Takeaways..239

Chapter 9 245

Mothers 245

Message to Mothers 249

Chapter 10 252

Lisa 252

Let's Recap 257

Chapter 10 261

Empaths 261

How to Tell if You're an Empath 265

Key Takeaways 269

Chapter 12 272

Shawn 272

Let's Recap 276

Chapter 13 280

Helping Professionals 280

Chapter 14 285

Toya 285

Chapter 15 302

Prioritizing Self-care: Non-negotiable 302

Beware of Falling Off the Track 308

So, How Do We Stay on Course When it Comes to Self-care? ... 310

Key Takeaways 315

Chapter 16 319

A Better Version of Me..319

Overcoming anxiety...320

Overcoming stress..321

11:11 My Purpose...325

Introduction

Hello and welcome! You are going to love it here in my beautiful world of self-care. Take a seat. Relax. Allow yourself to rest your shoulders and unclench your jaw. Take a deep breath. Exhale slowly. Now, let's begin. I am LaToya D. Thomas, better known as Toya and quite often referred to as Mom or Mommy. I will be your host as we travel together, exploring the rollercoaster-like chain of events I experienced, enabling me the wonderful opportunity to be here with you. It would later become these wild adventures, twists, and turns in life that equipped me with the knowledge, skills, and wisdom to write this book. As you read and reflect on your own experiences, I invite you to begin a self-care journey of your own. Don't worry. You are not alone. I will be here to guide you along the way. Allow me to set the tone so you know what to expect.

First and foremost, this is a judgment-free zone. Here, we will practice what it means to be gentle with ourselves. Why? For no other reason than because we deserve it. And let's go one step further to say we owe it to ourselves. That's right! Let's practice being as kind, gentle, and loving to ourselves as we are to those around us. Now, locate your oxygen mask and buckle up for the ride. No, this isn't a plane ride, but it is pretty interesting how life can be as unpredictable and turbulent as a plane flying through a storm.

If you have an *aha* moment while reading, feel free to use the notes section at the end of each chapter and take note of that moment. I encourage you to use this book interactively for both reading and writing. Let it help you to notice where barriers may exist in your life, not so much in the form of an actual fence or a wall, but mentally, physically, and emotionally. You may realize you have a few mental blocks you didn't know existed. While reading this book, you will learn helpful tips and acquire valuable, life-changing tools. For example, I will teach you the secret to fitting self-care into your overly-packed schedule. Some of our schedules are so full that adding one more thing to our list, or multiple lists, feels impossible. Don't worry; I have the perfect solution for this problem.

If you've purchased the *Self-care: A Better Version of Me Workbook,* you can follow along while reading as the workbook was designed to be used simultaneously. It is not necessary to have the workbook to reap the benefits of reading the book. However, since reading the book will invoke a plethora of feelings and inspirational moments, using both congruently will provide the best experience. Moreover, if you finish reading *this* book and later find that you would like to use the workbook to help guide your self-care journey, the workbook can be used as a stand-alone product.

Perhaps you're here reading this book, and you don't have any barriers. You may have made it a priority to practice self-care for quite some time now. Well, no worries. There is something for you as well. We can all benefit from reminders every now and then. Also, I challenge you to review your self-care routine and spruce it up. Since self-care looks and feels different to each of us, I have dedicated an entire chapter to identifying what self-care looks like for you. We will explore over 100 ways to practice self-care. I also offer tips on squeezing in a bit of me-time, even during those busy days when your schedule has reached capacity.

Whether you're a busy parent, an empath, a professional in a "helping field" (i.e., a physician, therapist, psychologist, psychiatrist, counselor, teacher, etc.), or someone who wants to learn more ways to become a better version of yourself, there is something here for you. The truth is, there is something here for everyone. I've realized that practicing self-care has no age limits, body type specifications, gender, or job requirements. It's a practice or set of practices that goes a long way in making us feel more fulfilled, more at peace, and content with our choices in life.

As you read, you'll realize that I often switch between telling my personal story and deep-diving into specific topics, giving some advice based on what I have learned along the way. I will share a lot about myself throughout this journey. You will also notice that most chapters end with *Key Takeaways*. The purpose of the *Key Takeaways* is to serve as reminders of the most critical messages within the chapter. Compare what you find to be the most important to what I have found to be most important and see how our ideas align.

So, who am I? And why did I write this book? For starters, I am a mother bear of three baby bears. Their ages range from 4 years old to 18 years old. I know! It's a wide gap. All I can say is that life has a funny way of happening. I could tell the tale of how that happened, but we might need another book for just that story alone or perhaps an adult beverage. It's a wild one.

I inserted my *Author Bio* at the back of the book in case you'd like the professional version of me. But here, in these pages, I wanted to share the raw, uncut version of myself, the one who had to experience ups and downs to get where I am today.

Those experiences taught me what it means to desperately need to practice self-care. I understand what it means for a person to lose themselves. I know because I lived it. Best of all, I learned that making subtle life changes and restructuring your schedule can play a huge role in finding yourself again.

Here is a little about me for those who may not want to wait to read the back of the book. For nearly 20 years, I worked with children and families. I was assigned to work with children who had special needs. Some were diagnosed with mental health disorders, and some were too young to be diagnosed at the time. I also worked with neurotypical children. While doing so, I had the amazing opportunity to help mothers who suffered from postpartum depression and a range of other illnesses. I provided assistance and support to these women and children as needed. Each family's needs varied greatly, as did my duties and responsibilities. My goal was always to help out as much as I could; to be a sense of relief for the families.

During that time, I received an associate degree in early childhood education. I'd hoped to open a childcare center at some point. As time passed, I attempted to leave the helping field and switch careers entirely, but I felt compelled to stay in many ways, so I did. I later felt a strong urge to continue my education. I loved learning! I still love learning. While searching for a college program that worked with my lifestyle and scheduling needs, I couldn't decide which major to choose. I gravitated toward psychology, sociology, and human services. I had ties to each of them. While psychology was my dream, sociology, which I initially loathed during my previous college experience, had recently become my new interest and grabbed my attention more and more. As for Human Services, I'd spent over a decade working in the field and held the idea of helping people in the community very close to my heart. At first, the decision-making process was challenging. However, the Behavioral Science program at Bellevue University, which focuses on all three subjects, was the answer to my indecision. I enrolled immediately upon finding their program. A short time later, I was incredibly proud to graduate from Bellevue University with a 4.0 GPA and a bachelor's degree in behavioral science.

I continued to work with children and families for a while after graduating. Actually, it was another two years, a pregnancy, and a global pandemic that led me to stop. Wow! I hadn't looked at it that way before writing this book, but it's true. When you love what you do, or the fear of failure prevents you from stepping out on faith and trying new things, you stick with what you know. Maybe it was the fear of the unknown.

Does that sound familiar to you? Even if the very thing we are doing is the source of our stress, we often continue to do it. For some, it's a lack of awareness and not fully understanding the consequences of their behaviors. For others, it may be a struggle with addiction, mental health issues, societal pressures, personal circumstances, limited access to resources, or a limited or nonexistent support system. Without the proper resources, some of us fall victim to being a creature of habit, even when it doesn't serve us well.

The problem with allowing the familiarity of our behaviors to dictate our actions, even when it doesn't benefit us emotionally, mentally, or physically, is that we do ourselves a disservice. We tend to get comfortable being uncomfortable. Eventually, our bodies become sick and tired, and before long, we find ourselves in even more uncomfortable places or, worse, unfamiliar and potentially dangerous mental spaces. This leads me to the first topic I'd like to discuss: burnout and pouring from an empty cup.

Chapter 1

Burnout: Pouring from an Empty Cup

A s I sat in the doctor's office cold and confused, I vividly remember feeling overwhelmed after getting a routine exam. I remember the nurse practitioner asking if I had thoughts of harming myself or anyone else. "Is she asking if I am having suicidal thoughts?" I wondered. I found the question extremely alarming. I was shocked and, honestly, a bit disturbed. I wondered why everything I had just shared led her to ask *that* question. So, let me rewind a bit.

I had two children at the time: a five-year-old girl and a one-year-old boy. My daughter was in kindergarten, and my son attended daycare full-time. Both of my children participated in some form of activity, and often, it was more than one activity per child. My daughter loved her group swim lessons and tolerated ballet. At the same time, my son participated in swim lessons, and since he was only a year old, when he had swim lessons, it meant that *we* took swim lessons together.

I was a single mother working a stressful full-time job and doing my best to provide for my children. I am not pointing that out for a pity party. There are some beautiful parts about being alone that we will dive into a little later. Instead, I point it out to emphasize the number of responsibilities I had and how fully loaded my plate was during that time.

I worked between 45-50 hours per week. Working with children who had special needs was a bit draining. Let me rephrase that. It was incredibly draining and often seemed to take all the energy I had in me, both physically and mentally, and many times emotionally, too. That's better; much more realistic.

After work, I would race to the after-school program to pick up my daughter. I'd hurry past the staff, who usually had a great story to tell, one that I barely had enough time to hear. It wasn't that I had no interest; instead, I was so busy trying to make it out of the door only to resume my race to the next destination, this time to the daycare to pick up my son before 6:00 p.m. when the late pickup charges would begin. One dollar per minute can feel like a lot when you're struggling financially. Let's not forget the guilt and the speed-walk-of-shame parents have after being late, yet again, due to the traffic or some other issue beyond their control. Some things are inevitable when you have a tight schedule and rush hour traffic to combat. That schedule was hectic, and it began to affect me mentally.

Once the children were with me, you might think the busyness of the day would end or at least slow down, that I could go home and have a peaceful evening with my two babies, and all would be well. Nope! It was quite the opposite. For some reason, I filled my mind with the idea that each child needed activities outside of school. Maybe it was the idea of socialization. Maybe it was for them to have fun or to learn an important life skill. Honestly, I don't know what I was thinking. I was so busy moving and keeping up with the schedule that I may have forgotten to think at all. Part of me wonders now if I was also attempting to keep up with the other parents in our neighborhood. See, my children weren't the only little busybodies around town. It was common for the other children in our neighborhood to be just as busy as my children were, maybe even a little more. They all had full schedules, and all of us moms were racing to keep up.

Because my first two children are four years apart, they have always attended different schools. The same applies to camps, sports, and almost every other activity. As for swimming, different lessons for different age groups also meant they would have lessons on different days of the week. Instead of rushing to swim lessons one day each week, to be fair to both children, it became two days of swim lessons per week. Before you think to yourself, *'Couldn't you have scheduled both lessons on the same day?'* I'll tell you now. The answer is no. As much as I had hoped for that level of convenience, the option was nonexistent.

Let's not forget dinner, homework, bathtime, bedtime routines, and me-time. Please take note of the placement of me-time and how it came last. Well, after a day like the ones I just described, which happened twice each week and again on ballet days, there was no time for me-time. Mama was exhausted!

So, as I sat on the table in the doctor's office, placing heavy emphasis on how tired I felt and, in hindsight, oversharing just a bit, the nurse practitioner could sense my exhaustion from the life I had created. She felt my frustration and probably noticed my apparent overwhelm. Now that I think about it, I poured it all out on that table. I don't think I held anything back. No wonder she asked if I felt suicidal. At the time, I thought she was overreacting, and her questions and concerns were a bit much. After all, I was used to complaining to other people who also complained about the same things. It was a mutual complainership, if you will. Yes, I made that word up, and no, I did not realize how toxic it was at the time. Generally, I would leave those conversations somehow feeling a slight sense of relief by knowing that we were all in the same boat and having the same experiences. I never really had anyone ask how I felt mentally, and I didn't know how to receive or process that level of concern.

"I said I am overworked, underpaid, and tired, not that I want to harm myself or my children," I thought to myself. When I think about it now, I understand. Just as I felt her questions were extreme, to her, the way I described my everyday life experiences and the pessimistic views I shared must have felt equally as extreme. My words were intense and heavy enough to alarm her, enough for her to question if I could be a danger to myself.

That day, my nurse said something I would never forget. Before diagnosing me with depression, she said, "Your problem is that you are only one person doing the jobs of two or more people, and you actually think you should be feeling normal." I never looked at it that way before. I really had been doing the jobs of multiple people on a daily basis, and I really thought it was normal. After all, it *was* my version of normal. After all I had shared during the visit, my nurse said she thought I should have been exhausted long before that moment. She was not at all surprised by my feeling of being overwhelmed and frustrated.

Later, when I thought about it, it made complete sense. I was overworked, stressed, completely worn out, stretched too thin, and now, freshly diagnosed with depression. *"How could this be?"* I thought. *"I am the fixer. I am the person who helps other people who suffer from and cope with depression. I am not the person who is depressed."* It was a part of my job at the time to care for other people experiencing similar issues. It didn't make any sense for me to be experiencing this type of burnout. *Or* did it make perfect sense after all?

It turned out that I was completely burned out. For months, maybe even years, I had been pouring from an empty cup. I had known all along that my schedule was intense. I knew there weren't enough hours in a day for all the tasks I wanted and needed to do, yet I continued to do them. I thought these things needed to be done, and since I was the only adult in the home, I didn't have a choice. I never considered that there was a different way, that perhaps I was doing too much. I poured into the families at work. I poured into my own family. I poured and poured and continued to pour until I found myself still trying to pour, only now I was pouring from an empty cup. I had nothing left to give.

There I was with my newly revealed problem and no solution in sight. I needed to take some time to figure things out. I needed to think, plan, and strategize. I realized I had neglected significant parts of my life for far too long. It was time to begin practicing self-care!

What is burnout?

Burnout is a state of mental, physical, or emotional exhaustion brought on by prolonged or repeated stress. It often feels as if your stress is never-ending and can be accompanied by feelings of emptiness, apathy, fatigue, and hopelessness.

Disclaimer: It is important to note that this is not the only definition of burnout and does not fully encompass all there is to know about burnout. I am not a medical doctor, and this is not medical advice. If you are experiencing any symptoms that you feel could be the result of burnout, I recommend speaking to your doctor or care team so that they

can work with you one-on-one to get the help you
may need.

What causes burnout?
Burnout is most often caused by issues that arise in
the workplace or other areas of life. Here is a list of
everyday events that could lead to burnout.

In the home

- Caretaking
- Feelings of failure
- Following a purpose that does not align with
  who you are and what you're meant to do in
  life
- Keeping up with others
- Lack of support
- Not taking a break
- Parenting
- People pleasing
- Personal relationships
- Too many responsibilities

In the workplace

- Avoiding taking a break from work
  (Collecting and Hoarding Paid Time Off)

- Issues with coworkers
- Issues with a supervisor, manager, or member of leadership
- Taking on too much work for an extended period of time

Symptoms of Burnout/Untreated Burnout

While experiencing burnout, a person may feel a combination of the symptoms below. Unrecognized and untreated burnout can lead to the following:

- Anger
- Annoyance
- Anxiety disorders
- Depression or Depressive symptoms
- Detachment
- Frustration
- Hopelessness
- Irritability
- Reduced Productivity
- Restlessness
- Sadness

The lists above are not complete, as there are more causes and symptoms of burnout. However, these are some of the most common causes and symptoms.

- **Share your feelings with your medical care team.**
Finding a physician with whom you will feel comfortable enough to build a relationship and share personal information about yourself is essential. Your nurse/doctor is a member of your care team and can only support you as much as you are willing to allow. If I had kept quiet during my visit to the doctor's office that day, I would likely be telling a completely different story.

  While there are numerous benefits to being transparent with your care team, one significant benefit is the many resources that may be available to you. We only know what we know, but when we share what we are experiencing with the right people, meaning people we know, trust, and know will have our best interests in mind, we open a world of possibilities, resources, help, support, and relief.

- **Talk to someone.**

If you are experiencing stress, overwhelm, anxiety, or burnout, find someone you trust and share your thoughts with that person. Life can be extremely challenging, and while in my case, I was not having suicidal thoughts, many people either have in the past or are currently in a deep, dark place and could use help. If you do not have anyone you can talk to and you are experiencing thoughts of harming yourself or others, please do not hesitate to contact the National Suicide Prevention Lifeline at 1-800-273-talk (8255), call or text 988 (Suicide & Crisis Lifeline), or even call 911.

- **Learn to recognize when your plate is too full.**
  Sometimes, we are overly ambitious and pile our plates a little too high. By plates, I am referring to our to-do lists, workloads, or the events on our calendars. You may find yourself people-pleasing, saying yes to every invite either because you don't want to hurt anyone's feelings, you don't want to miss out on any fun, or maybe you genuinely want to make it to every event. Be careful of adding

what may seem like just a few more tasks to an already overcrowded calendar.

Before saying yes or making additional commitments, check your schedule. Be realistic when deciding if what you are about to add to your list makes sense for you at that time or if it may be in your best interest to either wait or skip it altogether. Realize that you are amazing, but as extraordinary as you are, you are still only one person and can only take on so much at once.

- **Know that burnout is real.**
  Burnout occurs when a person is mentally, physically, or emotionally exhausted. Often caused by excessive or prolonged stress, burnout can lead to anxiety disorders, detachment, depression, and so much more. While experiencing burnout, one may feel a loss of motivation or hopelessness. These symptoms may worsen if left untreated. Help is available. Please do not hesitate to reach out to your medical care team, a family member, or a close friend.

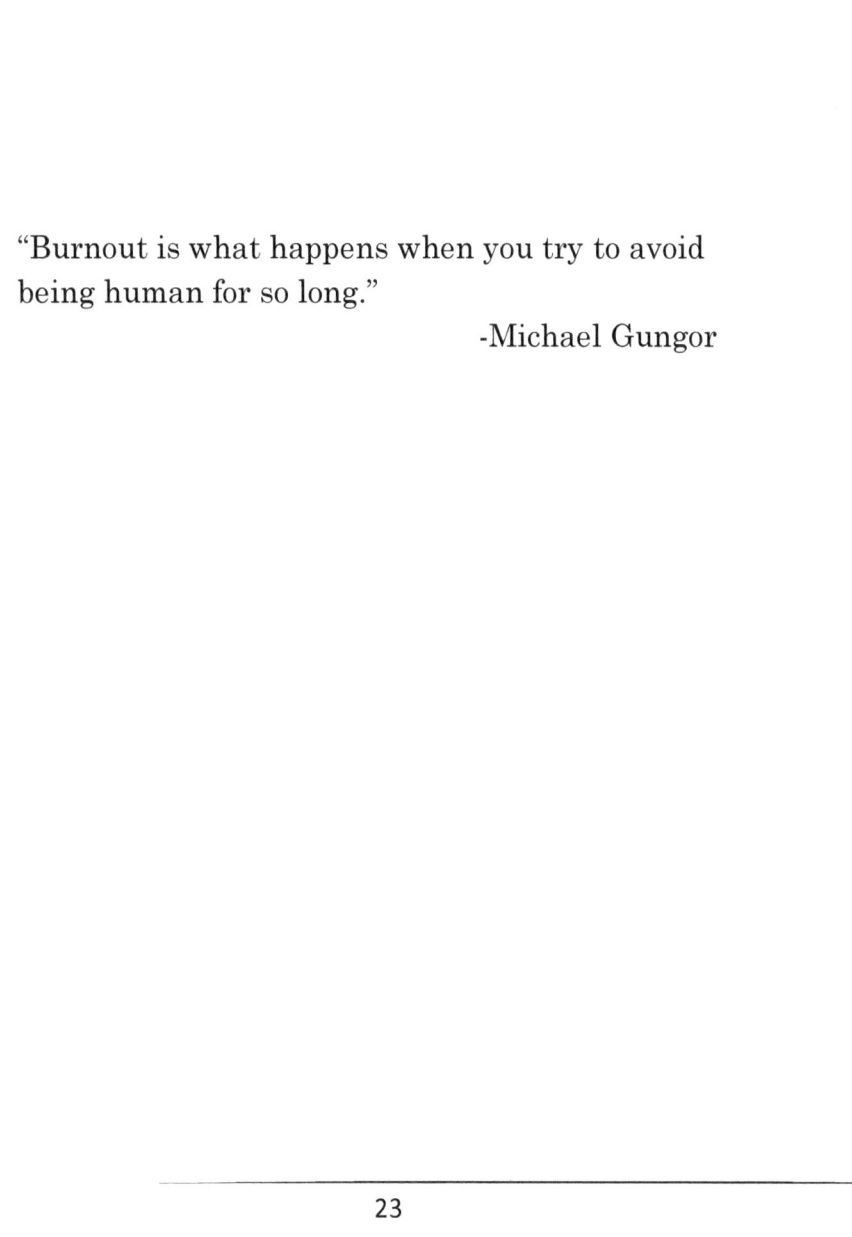

"Burnout is what happens when you try to avoid being human for so long."

-Michael Gungor

Notes

It is expected that as you read this book and reflect on your life, you'll have what I refer to as "Aha moments." These moments are comparable to light bulbs being turned on, or dots being connected that seem to suddenly make past events or thoughts make sense. They may make you say, "Aha!"

A notes section appears at the end of each chapter and is intended to allow readers to interact as they read this personal development self-help book. Jot down your thoughts, memorable quotes, aha moments, or any ideas, feelings, or emotions you may experience. If you would rather read without stopping to write notes, that is perfectly fine, too.

Notes

Notes

Chapter 2

Identifying Barriers

Before we can fix a problem, we need to know it exists. Taking time to learn the source of our problems will also help to identify our barriers. A barrier is *anything* that prevents us from moving forward. It can be a person, a place, a thing, a thought, a set of circumstances, a set of beliefs, or anything else that impedes growth or progress. Barriers act as obstacles and can vary in size. They can affect us in a multitude of ways. In the worst cases, a barrier can prevent a person from reaching their full potential, and they never live to see or experience the best version of themselves. Some people know their barriers, while others are completely oblivious. Let's explore various types of barriers so you know what to look out for when you are ready to begin your journey of self-discovery and self-awareness.

When your barrier is a limiting belief system or lack of resources

We rarely sit and analyze our belief systems to determine if they make sense and fit our current lifestyles or if our inherited beliefs from childhood no longer serve us. While we know beliefs other than our own exist, we somehow hold firmly to what we believe without considering if our beliefs are logical. People become so emotionally invested in their beliefs that many resort to anger and frustration to support or prove their beliefs should also be those of others. However, when we grow and evolve, so should our belief systems.

Take politics as an example. The world is so divided on politics-related topics that people have lost close friends during presidential elections. Religion is equally controversial, if not more, than politics. Some people will not associate with people from a religion that they believe is wrong, evil, or just different from their own. There are also less serious topics that people feel equally strongly about, such as sports teams, food preferences, occupations, and goals.

Our beliefs direct us in almost every step we take and everything we do. What we believe dramatically influences how we think, what we allow, what we deem acceptable and unacceptable, and how we react to others and the world around us.

On the topic of the world, isn't it interesting to think that there are approximately 7.9 billion people in this gigantic world? I know. That was random and may seem a little off topic. But not really. Let me explain. When it comes to recognizing our barriers and problem-solving, we often try a few different methods and then stop. After we've tried everything that initially comes to mind, we conclude that we've tried everything. From time to time, we may get a little help from a family member or a friend, that is, if we aren't too prideful. With their help, we think of a few more options for solving the problem. Feeling a new sense of hope, we try their suggestions, and if their way doesn't work, we officially declare that we have tried everything.

It is mind-boggling how quickly we give up on our ideas, deeming them impossible when we think we cannot achieve them. We all have something to contribute to this world starting from birth, if not earlier. When we are born, we become the newest members of our families. Our families, yours and mine, are members of a community. Our communities, along with other communities, combine to make a neighborhood. Our neighborhood is in a city or town located in a state or country somewhere in the world. I know this is a lot, but stay with me, and it will all begin to make sense. It all started with us being a single member of a single family.

Have you ever heard anyone say:

"I've tried everything, literally, everything."

"Nothing works for me."

"I give up. Maybe it isn't for me."

"It didn't work for me. Maybe it's my bad luck."

We have all heard some variations of these statements. Often, when people are frustrated and hopelessly out of options, they utter these words or something similar. Sometimes, our previous life experiences can lead us to believe that such statements are factual, but as I mentioned, there are nearly 7.9 billion people in this world as I write this book. I find it impossible to believe that any one individual who attempts to problem-solve on their own will have truly tried everything there is to try at the end of their attempt. It is equally as impossible to believe that there is no resolution whatsoever for whatever issues one may be experiencing. There is always a way to work through a problem and break barriers, even if it initially doesn't seem obvious.

As we identify our barriers, we may discover that the people in our lives have held us back. It's a terrible realization to learn that a family member who loves you may also be the person who is responsible for hindering your progress. It could be someone from your past or currently in your life.

It is important to note that when we consult with our family and friends, each person's advice and suggestions stem from their beliefs, experiences, biases, and fears. Taking advice from someone whose advice is unknowingly based on fear, misconceptions, or inaccuracies can lead to your own limited beliefs and can act as a significant barrier.

People-Pleasing

From a young age, parents plan their children's future. They orchestrate the child's life, attempting to influence almost every decision until the child reaches an age where they can take over the decision-making process. However, this stage in life can be challenging for both the young adult and the parent. As a parent, letting go can be extremely challenging. Some parents push their children to follow the path they imagined, and when the child becomes an adult and chooses a different path, they feel hurt, disappointed, discouraged, and a host of other emotions. Depending on the parent's reaction, a child may attempt to please their parent even if their parent's visions do not align with their own. This behavior can lead the child, who is no longer a child, to begin a life of people-pleasing, which is doing what someone else would like them to do to make them happy, even if it isn't what they want to do. People-pleasing can begin in childhood and can last an entire lifetime. The problem arises when pleasing others impedes the pleaser's goals, wishes, and dreams.

Sometimes, the person who feels the need to please their parents turns into the person who needs to please their friends and coworkers, the stranger at the mall, and everyone else they encounter. Living up to everyone else's expectations can be a huge barrier.

Social Expectations

Pressure to conform to society's expectations can leave a person feeling inadequate, empty, stressed, and depressed. The bad news is that is how much of the world operates. The good news is if you're feeling this way, you may not have found your people yet, and there is hope. When you find your people, I mean the ones who understand you and are just like you, there is much less pressure to meet unnecessary expectations or feel out of place.

Additionally, when you begin to make positive changes that may not benefit those around you and when you refocus your attention, people will notice. Hopefully, you have supportive family and friends, and when they see you making time for yourself or living in your purpose, whatever that may be, they cheer and shout, "I love that for you!" But if you are like most of us, you may encounter those family and friends who simply do not understand why you need time to yourself, why you need to follow a different path, why you may not be able to commit to a task they need you to do, or why you may need to say no. Some people may even take offense as you reallocate your time to begin the much-needed work of focusing on yourself.

Toxic Associations & Unhealthy Relationships

We all know them. You know, those friends who never have anything good to say, that colleague who loves to complain about everything from her commute to her children, her in-laws, and everything in between, and we cannot forget the family member who only calls for one of two reasons: to gossip or to ask for a favor. Toxic people are everywhere. It is best to maintain a healthy distance from these types of people. Unhealthy relationships can be poisonous, and these relationships can drain your energy. If you are not careful, you could begin to focus on the half-empty glass.

Let's briefly dive into the classic glass-half-full or half-empty proverbial phrase. I assume most readers will recognize this reference, but I will explain quickly for those who don't know. Imagine there is a glass sitting on a table in front of you. The glass can hold eight ounces of liquid and currently contains four ounces of water. Would you consider the glass half-full or half-empty? How you answer this question says a lot about you.

Some of us grew up in homes where the glass would be considered half-empty. If the person who views the glass as half-empty visits a friend and the friend offers them a glass of water and fills it halfway, the person who views the glass as half-empty may feel slightly offended, angry, disappointed, and other negative emotions. This person is likely to create negative, irrational reasons for why the person would only fill the glass halfway.

They may think to themselves:

"'Maybe they don't want me to have the water."

"Maybe they don't want to share. How cheap or selfish!"

"Maybe they don't really like me, or maybe they don't really want me here."

As you can see, the perspective of the person who sees the glass as half-empty is likely to be negative. Then, there is the flip side. The person who sees the glass as half-full will have an entirely different perspective. They may graciously accept the water with gratitude and never wonder about the amount of water in the cup. Or, if they do take notice of the amount of water, they may think:

"Maybe they are conscious about wasting water."

"If the glass was full, there is a chance I would not drink the entire glass of water anyway."

"I can always get more if I am still thirsty."

"I am grateful for what I've received."

This way of thinking is more appreciative, accepting, forgiving, compassionate, and thoughtful. It's positive. While this is just one example, it is similar to how we handle other thoughts and beliefs. This is also an excellent example of why watching the company you keep is crucial. If the majority of your friends are "glass half-empty" thinkers, there is a chance that you are, too.

We often limit ourselves based on what we believe to be true. Our thoughts become barriers, and if they go unchecked or unmanaged, we can keep ourselves from truly reaching our maximum level of fulfillment, happiness, and potential. There are many ways people can adopt limiting belief systems. Sometimes, unlearning those beliefs is one of the best parts of life. It can open so many doors.

We've discussed limiting beliefs related to family and friends and when your barriers may be a person or a group of people. However, we must be realistic with ourselves. Sometimes, we cannot blame other people. What I am about to say next can be a harsh reality, but sometimes, as sad as it may sound, the person holding you back is you.

When Your Barrier is You

Here is a list of ways we can be our own barrier without realizing it, or maybe you know it but haven't taken action to resolve the problem. Either way, if you discover that you have been the person impeding your own progress, I have great news! It's never too late to start being better than you were yesterday.

1. **Negative Self-Talk**
   Persistent negative inner dialogue or
   thoughts about yourself can be a barrier.
   Negative self-talk can lead to low self-esteem
   and a lack of motivation. If there is
   something you don't like about yourself, first,
   let me tell you that it's perfectly normal to
   have both likes and dislikes about yourself.
   You, my friend, are human.

What I learned when I worked with children
and families and from countless
conversations I've had with women of all
ages, ethnicities, body types, and
socioeconomic statuses is that we are all
alike at the end of the day. We all have
insecurities and want to be the best versions
of ourselves, even if we struggle to do so.

I spoke with women with straight hair who
would do anything to have curly hair. I knew
women with curly hair who hated it and
wished they had straight hair. I met tall
women who wished they were short and
short women who would kill to be three
inches taller. I had conversations with people

who wanted to gain weight and many discussions with those who struggled with weight and wished they were thinner. I even spoke with young girls who felt they needed to go on diets at the ages of preteens and teens. It seemed to me that no one was happy with who they were. Ultimately, it was these conversations, paired with a personal conversation with my own daughter, who voiced concerns about her complexion being too dark at the age of nine, that led me to publish my first book, which is a children's book titled "You Are Beautiful, Beautiful You Are."

In my children's book, I speak to young children to encourage them to accept the unique features that make them who they are because each of us is special in our own way. I tell children to love themselves and others. When I wrote the book, I felt fewer adults would be filled with so many negative thoughts about themselves if I could reach children while they are young. A page in the book repeats itself with hopes of drilling the message into their minds. The message read, "You are beautiful, beautiful you are." So, if you're a person who looks in the mirror and doesn't like what you see, or if you constantly tell yourself that you are not worthy or you cannot do something or any negative self-talk, I am here to tell you, "You are beautiful, beautiful you are." You are amazing! Remember that.

2. **Focusing on Negativity**
   It's no secret that some people are drawn to drama. It's like they are drama magnets; drama literally comes to knock on their door every morning, and it finds them. There's a reason for that. What we focus on is what we will get. If you go outside and look for red cars, you will find red cars. Then, you'll notice that red cars are everywhere you go. You will begin to spot a red car before it turns the corner. Why? Because you focused on it. The same is true for drama and negativity. If you entertain every negative conversation, you'll soon find yourself having more negativity in your life than you ever imagined, but guess what? The same is also true for positivity. If you begin to focus on positivity and slowly, or quickly, eliminate

negativity, you'll find that life is so much better on the positive side.

Going from positive to negative can be a challenge. You may feel as if you don't know how to be positive. You may need to figure out what to say or do or how to fit in. If you're from a place where negativity is the way of life, it can be even more challenging. For example, if you're in school or working a job where complaining is typical, or maybe you are a member of a group, or maybe you're on social media, the home of drama, or maybe you watch the local or international news regularly, or maybe you gossip with your best friend or sister daily. All of these can be considered negative and can act as a barrier in your life. Why? It is incredibly challenging to focus on yourself and your own life, fulfilling your own bucket list if you're also focused on everyone else and what they have going on. One of the best ways to stop focusing on negativity is to start focusing on positivity, goals, and your new self-care journey.

3. **Perfectionism**

   Perfectionism is a belief that something or someone must be or appear perfect, without flaws, or to believe in the possibility of such a thing. This way of thinking may create unrealistic expectations, causing stress in the pursuit of unattainable standards. Perfection simply does not exist unless we alter the meaning a bit. Most perfectionists know this, yet we still strive for perfection. It can be problematic and can even prevent one from reaching their goals. To change the meaning of the word perfect is to accept things and people with their flaws and to be okay with that.

   My friend Anna used to tell me, "Toya, it's better to be finished than perfect." Anna, if you're reading this, I love you to pieces, and you're the best! I also had a CEO I worked with tell me about the 80/20 rule. He said, "Don't spend 80% of the time working on the last 20% of the project." The reality is that the details may not matter to anyone besides you, the perfectionist. The next time you find yourself knee-deep in an attempt to make yourself or something else perfect, remind yourself that it's fine just the way it is, and then stop. Whatever it is, especially if it's you, it's probably perfect in its current state, not to mention that there is something so beautiful about people, places, and things being perfectly imperfect anyway. No one needs unrealistic expectations or unnecessary stress.

4. **Lack of Awareness**

We only know what we know. The more we learn, the more we may realize how little we actually know. Sometimes, we unintentionally hold ourselves back simply because we don't know any better. This is why it's essential to read, explore, learn new things, and get outside of your comfort zone. You never know what the world has to offer you if all you do is work, come home to sleep, and repeat the cycle the next day. I encourage everyone to become more involved and aware. Think of something you want to learn more about and go after it.

5. **Lack of Motivation**
   Finding motivation can be challenging at
   times and easier at other times. We are all
   motivated by different things, and it can be a
   struggle to get it back when we lose
   motivation. During hard times, remember to
   focus on your why. When you have a reason
   that is powerful enough and surround
   yourself with the right people, scenery, and
   other forms of motivation, you may find it
   easier to get the boost you need.

   Sometimes, unexpected life events can take
   us for a loop. We may find that something
   that once motivated us and brought us joy is
   no longer interesting at all. There are times
   when we can easily get back on track, but
   there are also times when we need to speak
   with someone to gain a better understanding
   of what we are experiencing. Never ignore
   when you feel like something deeper could be
   going on, as having a lack of motivation is a
   beginning sign that one could be
   experiencing stress, burnout, depression,
   anxiety, and much more.

6. Being close-minded

One could be close-minded for various reasons. It could be their ingrained beliefs or a strong desire to maintain a sense of stability. It could also be fear: fear of the unknown, fear of upsetting the people around them, or fear of failure. Many people are afraid of change. Following a schedule and knowing exactly how the day will pan out can be very comforting until it isn't anymore. Sometimes, following the same schedule day after day can leave a person feeling unenthused and bored, and could leave a person feeling unfulfilled. If you are close-minded with specific topics, it is worth exploring what those topics are and why you feel so strongly about them. You may find it's not as bad, different, or scary as you imagined.

Other Types of Barriers

There are so many categories of barriers. You'll notice that the following list may also fit in the previous categories but can also fit into others, so they landed here. Regardless of the category, it is important to note these and any other barriers you may notice or experience in your life or the lives of the people around you.

1. **Unreasonable expectations**
   We touched on this a little with the perfectionists. However, there are other times and other people who may have unrealistic expectations. You may see this regarding relationships, careers, or personal achievements. Society, social media, TV, movies, or personal insecurities may influence these unrealistic expectations.

2. **Time Constraints**
   Busy schedules and hectic lifestyles can certainly be a barrier. Not having enough time might be one of the most used excuses in the world. There is no doubt that having a robust schedule can get in the way of allocating time for self-care or other essential activities.

3. **Lack of Boundaries**
   Have you ever felt you needed to set better boundaries with yourself or the people

around you? Difficulty establishing and maintaining personal boundaries can lead to overcommitment and neglect of self-care. Learning to set boundaries can be one of the best lessons ever. Protect your time. Protect your peace.

4. **Financial Constraints**
Limited resources, financial or otherwise, can be restricting and may cause a person to need to be more strategic, careful, or frugal than someone who does not have financial constraints. Not having enough money can lead to feelings of inadequacy, disappointment, anger, and discouragement.

5. **Overwhelming Responsibilities & Multitasking**
No offense to anyone else, but if you are a mother, there is a good chance that you are a multitasking professional. You may not have always been that way, and maybe you were never good at it before, but there is something about motherhood that instantly gives us multitasking capabilities. There are certainly other people who fit the

multitasking queen and king category. It's a gift, and it can also be a curse. Have you ever juggled numerous responsibilities simultaneously, and everyone around you thought you were amazing yet didn't feel amazing? Instead, you probably felt horrible, tired, overworked, underpaid, and maybe even fed up.

What happened to taking one step at a time, starting small, working your way up, and finishing one thing before starting another? Instead, we push ourselves to the point of exhaustion, never stopping to ask for help or to realize that there is another way. And to top it off, there is a good chance that we are not leaving any time for self-care, so we continue to deplete ourselves. That can be a massive barrier because we eventually realize we're doing so much that nothing is being done correctly. We aren't giving the best of ourselves to any one area, so instead of feeling like conquerors, we feel defeated. We are going to work on that, right? Yes, we can multitask, but even if we remove one task from our plate, let's call it a win. Then, let's begin to be more realistic with what we allow ourselves or others to put back on the plate. If they want to remove something, great, but let's be mindful of adding things, tasks, and events to an already full plate.

6. All-or-Nothing Thinking

Viewing any topic as an all-or-nothing endeavor is similar to seeing the world as only black-and-white and forgetting about the gray areas that lie somewhere in the middle. This way of thinking can act as an unnoticed barrier. Some people think they should not do anything if they cannot do it all. Taking no action at all stops progress completely, but taking small, actionable, and consistent actions toward achieving the goal can be much more advantageous. If you cannot accomplish the bigger goal right now, start small with a more achievable goal. Doing so will help you get closer to the bigger goal. Remember, slow and steady wins the race.

7. **Guilt and Self-Sacrifice**
   Can we say it together? Self-care is not selfish. Self-care is not selfish. And one more time for the people in the back. Self-care is not selfish. Please do not allow yourself to believe that taking better care of yourself is a selfish act. In other chapters, we will explore self-care, the myths, and what self-care looks like for different people, but consider this an intro and a reminder that self-care is not selfish. Believing that prioritizing oneself is selfish or takes away from others can lead to neglecting your own personal needs and self-sacrificing. You cannot be your best when you don't take the time to care for yourself mentally, physically, and emotionally.

8. **Fixed Mindset**
   Believing that personal abilities and qualities are fixed traits can discourage efforts to learn and grow, which can be a really unfortunate barrier. A person's abilities, qualities, and even their level of intelligence are not static and can fluctuate. Having a fixed mindset can hinder personal growth if this way of thinking causes a person to avoid challenges, fear failure, and

limit their efforts. The flip side to the fixed mindset is the growth mindset, which allows for adaptability and a willingness to learn.

9. **Cognitive Distortions**
   Distorted thinking patterns, such as catastrophizing or overgeneralizing, can contribute to stress and hinder one's ability to see the world realistically. Catastrophizing is a cognitive distortion in which a person tends to imagine and focus on the worst possible outcomes of a situation. It involves magnifying or exaggerating the potential consequences to an unrealistic extent.

   Overgeneralizing is another cognitive distortion where people take minimal information, such as an isolated incident, and make broad, general statements based on that information. With overgeneralization, the person does not consider the full context or have evidence to support their conclusion.

10. Mental Health Challenges

It is important to know what is in your control and what is not. Dealing with mental health concerns can make it challenging to do even the smallest of tasks at times. If you are experiencing this, please don't be hard on yourself. Take one day at a time; if that feels too much, take it one hour at a time. Be gentle with yourself. You are already dealing with a lot. If you're able to set a goal and focus on it, be sure to set small, easily attainable goals. Try not to look at the bigger picture because it can be overwhelming for some people. If you need support, find an amazing support group, counselor, friend, or family member and get the support you need. Remember, you've got this!

When we begin to open our minds to think more realistically about ourselves and the world around us, we begin to break the barriers. Once you become aware of what's holding you back, your vision becomes clearer. Sometimes, our barriers are within our control and easy to break, and others are more complex. Either way, identifying them is the first step toward a better future, even if the discovery process brings feelings of ambivalence. Making discoveries can provoke a range of emotions that can be challenging to navigate.

What would happen if we widened our audience and options and involved people with different beliefs and those with completely different life experiences? What if we learn from people who are unbiased and unafraid? What if we venture outside of our usual circles and discover the opinions of even a fraction of a percentage of the 7.9 billion people in the world? Better yet, what if we conduct research and rely on factual data from experts? Could you imagine how different the perspective of someone other than your friends and family could be? If we could think outside of the world we know, our options would increase tremendously. The advice and opinions we receive would vary greatly, allowing us to make more informed decisions. Possibilities would be endless.

As for my own barriers, when my two older children were younger, I always felt guilty whenever I took time for myself. I didn't understand the importance or necessity of practicing self-care. I don't know what makes parents, particularly mothers, feel as if we are somehow neglecting our children when we tend to ourselves and our own needs. It's such an unhealthy way of thinking and a hugely limiting belief. Some of us believe one hundred percent of our time and attention should be spent on our children, taking care of their wants and needs, catering, and nurturing, or else we are labeled bad parents. But in reality, no reasonable person expects a mother to dedicate all her time or attention to parenthood. Is it us? Is it society? Is it what we think society would say? Or is it all in our heads? Hmm.

I was too busy to take the time to realize that piling more things on my to-do list was a terrible idea. If I had sat down and thought about it, perhaps I would have come to the realization that a one-year-old really didn't need swimming lessons in the dead of the winter after I had just worked 8-10 hours. Maybe it could have waited until spring or summer or maybe another year or two when life calmed down a little. Maybe my little ballerina could have skipped a ballet session. Maybe I could have saved the money from both activities to get a babysitter to assist with pickups and drop-offs as needed, which would have not only freed up time but would also decrease the inevitable stress and high blood pressure I ended up with as a result of the go-go-go lifestyle. But unfortunately, I was too far into the fog to be able to see through it. Of course, it all makes sense to me now that it's all in the past. As the saying goes, "hindsight is 20/20." If you have never heard that saying before, it means that you can see perfectly clearly when you look back at a situation after it has occurred.

Step one: Identify your barrier(s). Step two: Begin to do a little critical thinking to learn why the barrier(s) exist(s). Step three: Don't be surprised if this leads you down a rabbit hole of profound and unexpected discovery. Only once you begin your journey of self-discovery will you begin to strategize and learn how to break free and move toward becoming a better version of yourself. If you've purchased the *Self Care: A Better Version of Me Workbook*, there are exercises on identifying your barriers, increasing self-awareness, and self-discovery.

- **Identify your barriers.**

A barrier is *anything* that prevents us from moving forward. It can be a person, a place, a thing, a thought, a set of circumstances, a set of beliefs, or anything else that impedes growth or progress. Barriers are obstacles of varying sizes and can affect us in a multitude of ways.

A barrier can be any of the following:

- o Limiting belief systems
- o Lack of resources
- o A person or group of people
- o Yourself
- o Various other types

- **Discover why your barriers exist.**

Once you identify your barriers, the next step is discovering why they exist. There are many reasons why we have barriers, some stemming back to childhood. When you know the why, you can move toward finding a solution.

- **Help is available. You don't need to figure it out all by yourself.**

In the *Self Care: A Better Version of Me Workbook*, there are exercises and worksheets that cover identifying your barriers, increasing self-awareness, self-discovery, and much more.

Notes

Notes

Chapter 3

Self-Discovery

Have you taken time to assess who you are, who you once were, and who you would like to become? Do you feel you've grown or matured over the past five to ten years of your life? Was there a major life experience that changed you or changed the trajectory of your life? Usually, people know what makes them angry and can talk about it quickly and easily, but do you know the things that make you the happiest? What brings you joy? Pause for a minute and think of three things that make you happy. Are you regularly engaging in any of those things? If you have a hard time answering these questions, don't worry. By the end of this chapter, you will begin to think more about your life, your interests, your why, and your future. Through self-discovery and self-awareness, we learn so much about who we are and who we want to become. And to the person questioning whether it's too late or wondering if you're too old, I want you to know that it's never too late. You are never too old to learn, discover, become aware, or change for the better.

Self-Discovery

Self-discovery is the process of acquiring insight into one's true nature, character, and potential. It often involves uncovering aspects of ourselves that were previously unknown or unexplored. It's a journey of exploration involving various experiences, challenges, and moments of revelation. It may include discovering hidden talents, passions, or layers of a person's identity.

The goal of self-discovery is to explore deeper layers of ourselves and gain a more profound understanding of our aspirations, purpose, and potential. It often leads to personal transformation. The benefits of self-discovery include enhanced self-confidence, a clearer sense of purpose, and a more authentic, fulfilling life.

Self-Awareness

Self-awareness is the conscious knowledge of one's character, feelings, motives, and desires. It involves understanding ourselves in a reflective and introspective manner. Self-awareness is an ongoing process that requires introspection, self-reflection, and an honest assessment of thoughts, emotions, and behaviors.

Self-awareness is not something most of us practice daily. If you are a parent, you probably know all too well that there are times when you don't focus on yourself at all. However, self-awareness plays a significant role in the self-care journey, and it takes practice to become self-aware. To start, pay attention to your emotions. Take note of what makes you happy, what makes you feel sad, and every emotion in between. The *Image of Emotions* (pictured below) displays a wide range of emotions. Take a minute to review each emotion and think of the last time you felt each one. Who were you with when you felt these emotions? Where were you?

What were you doing? It's essential to stop the hustle and bustle of our busy lives and think about the answers to these questions. Sometimes, the answers to our problems are in plain sight, and we need to take time to notice them.

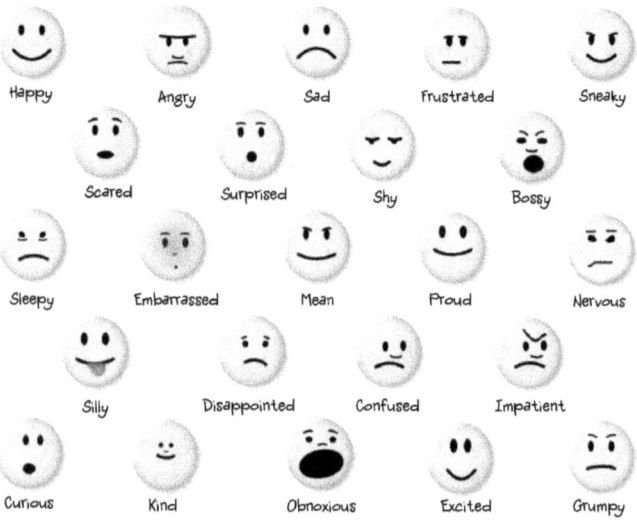

Image of Emotions

The primary goal of self-awareness is to gain a deeper understanding of your identity, strengths, weaknesses, values, and beliefs. It provides a foundation for personal growth and effective decision-making. The benefits of cultivating self-awareness include improved emotional intelligence, better communication, and the ability to make choices aligned with personal values.

Self-Discovery and Self-Awareness

Self-discovery and self-awareness are interconnected. Self-awareness can be considered a component of self-discovery, as becoming self-aware is a crucial step in the broader journey of self-discovery. Self-awareness focuses on understanding current thoughts, feelings, and behaviors. Self-discovery involves a more extensive exploration, uncovering aspects of ourselves that have not been revealed.

Self-awareness is a continuous process, while self-discovery may involve specific phases or periods of profound realization triggered by various life experiences. Self-awareness is often applied in the day-to-day management of emotions and decisions. Self-discovery, however, has a transformative impact on one's overall life direction and purpose. Both processes contribute to personal growth and a deeper understanding.

Key elements of self-discovery include:

- **Life Experiences**
  There is no doubt that life experiences shape us.
  Self-discovery teaches us to embrace diverse life
  experiences, both positive and challenging, and
  to view these experiences as opportunities for
  learning and self-awareness. Lessons can be
  learned from our success as well as from our
  setbacks.

- **Exploration of Passions and Interests**
  Actively engaging in activities that bring joy
  and fulfillment is important. Identifying and
  pursuing hobbies and interests that resonate
  with personal values can make a person feel
  whole, understood, and peaceful.

- **Facing Challenges and Adversity**
  Life is full of challenges and adversity.
  Navigating and overcoming challenges teaches a
  lot about who we are. Through challenges, we
  learn about resilience and inner strength.

- **Mindfulness and Present-Moment
  Awareness**
  Mindfulness allows us to stay present and fully
  experience the current moment. Through

practicing mindfulness, we develop awareness of our thoughts, emotions, and physical sensations.

- **Personal Values**

Identifying and understanding how your core personal values guide your decision-making and actions is a crucial step toward self-awareness. Aligning actions and choices with personal values is essential for living a more authentic life.

- **Goal Setting and Achievement**

Setting meaningful and achievable goals reflects personal aspirations. We should celebrate accomplishments, even for the small goals, and acknowledge personal growth.

- **Relationships and Social Dynamics**

Exploring and understanding interpersonal relationships and their impact on personal growth is crucial. Recognizing relationship patterns and learning about individual needs and boundaries is essential to living a well-balanced life.

- **Self-Expression**

Self-expression is engaging in creative outlets, such as writing, art, or music, and expressing thoughts and emotions freely. These outlets can feel liberating and help reduce stress.

- **Continuous Learning and Curiosity**
Embrace a mindset of continuous learning and curiosity regardless of your age. Seek knowledge and new experiences to expand your horizons.

- **Mind-Body Connection**
Recognizing the interconnectedness of mental and physical well-being is life changing. Explore practices that promote a harmonious mind-body relationship, such as exercise, meditation, or yoga. Know that it may take time to find what works for you. Don't allow previous experiences that didn't work well to end your path of exploration.

- **Spiritual Exploration**
Seek a sense of connection and purpose beyond the material aspects of life. Explore spiritual beliefs and practices that resonate with your personal values.

- **Self-Perception**
Self-perception refers to how individuals perceive and interpret themselves, including their thoughts, feelings, abilities, and overall identity. It plays a crucial role in shaping self-esteem, self-confidence, and overall well-being.
- **Acceptance and Self-Compassion**

Rule number one: Be kind to yourself. Kindness matters, especially when it comes to ourselves. Cultivate self-acceptance and compassion for your strengths and imperfections. Let go of self-judgment and embrace a positive self-image.

- **Reflection and Introspection**
Reflection and introspection involve taking time to gain insight and self-reflect, exploring thoughts, feelings, and experiences, and asking meaningful questions about personal values, beliefs, and aspirations.

Each person's journey of self-discovery is unique, and these elements may interconnect and overlap throughout the journey. Exploring these elements contributes to personal growth, a clearer sense of identity, and a more authentic and fulfilling life. If you've purchased the *Self-care: A Better Version of Me Workbook,* you will find an entire chapter dedicated to self-discovery. There are dozens of reflection and introspection questions that help with the self-discovery process. For those who do not have the *Self-care: A Better Version of Me Workbook,* here are a few examples of reflection and introspection questions to get you started:

Reflection questions
  1. What were the highlights of my week?

2. What challenges did I face? And how did I handle them?
3. In what ways did I step out of my comfort zone?

Introspection questions
1. What are my core values?
2. What self-limiting beliefs may be holding me back?
3. What are my personal boundaries? What are my professional boundaries? Do the people around me respect my boundaries?

Reflection and introspection are journeys within a journey, so I saved these two for last. When we reflect on our lives, we look back, not to harp on our mistakes or focus on our regrets, but instead, to direct our future. Yes, we think about what went wrong, but only so we can improve next time. From previous experiences, we learn our strengths and weaknesses. Introspection helps us to explore and improve areas such as emotional intelligence, self-perception, life purpose, interpersonal dynamics, and cultural awareness. The *Self-care: A Better Version of Me Workbook* has guided worksheets covering these topics. Surely, one could explore these topics on a solo mission. However, without guidance, it can be an overwhelming experience.

- Self-discovery is the process of acquiring insight into one's true nature, character, and potential. It often involves uncovering aspects of ourselves that were previously unknown or unexplored. It's a journey of exploration involving various experiences, challenges, and moments of revelation. It may include discovering hidden talents, passions, or layers of a person's identity.

- Self-awareness is the conscious knowledge of one's character, feelings, motives, and desires. It involves understanding ourselves in a reflective and introspective manner. Self-awareness is an ongoing process that requires introspection, self-reflection, and an honest assessment of thoughts, emotions, and behaviors.

- Key elements of self-discovery include:
  o Life Experiences
  o Exploration of Passions and Interests
  o Facing Challenges and Adversity
  o Mindfulness and Present-Moment Awareness
  o Personal Values
  o Goal Setting and Achievement
  o Relationships and Social Dynamics
  o Self-Expression

- o Continuous Learning and Curiosity
- o Mind-Body Connection
- o Spiritual Exploration
- o Self-Perception
- o Acceptance and Self-Compassion
- o Reflection and Introspection

- All topics covered in this chapter are also covered in great detail in the *Self-care: A Better Version of Me Workbook.*

Notes

Notes

Chapter 4

Ciara

Meet Ciara! Ciara is a fourth-grade teacher working in a suburban elementary school. Work is rewarding some days but stressful most other days. Because she doesn't finish her lesson planning and grading during the regular school day, Ciara spends time in the evening trying to catch up and get it all done. She has a child and struggles with balancing parenthood, work life, the little social life she manages to squeeze into her schedule, and self-care. Ciara believes she has tried everything to create some sense of balance, and nothing has worked.

Out of frustration, Ciara complained to her family about her problems with balancing life. Her mother offered motherly advice that wasn't necessarily helpful. She would often make the following statements:

"Make sure you take care of yourself."

"You need to take some time for yourself."

"Health is wealth!"

Her sister, who had two children slightly older than Ciara's child, totally understood what she was going through. She empathized as much as she could, but there was always that feeling of comparison between Ciara's complaints of having one child and working and herself having two children. The sister didn't fully understand how someone with one child could struggle as much as Ciara claimed to struggle. Her sister would unintentionally solicit guilt-ridden comments, such as, "Imagine if there were two" or "I wish I could go back to having just one. Those were the easy days." Both comments minimized Ciara's experiences, so she didn't feel as if her sister was a great person to vent to since she always turned it into making Ciara feel like she should appreciate how easy she has it with just one child.

It didn't stop there. Ciara was from a large family. Any and all news traveled fast. Her sister spoke with their aunt, and before Ciara knew it, her aunt and two cousins were all calling, offering more advice than Ciara wanted or needed. Between the three of them, Ciara heard:

"You need a vacation."

"You need to stop coddling that baby and let him be more independent. Maybe that's the problem."

"I don't know how you do it. It couldn't be me. How can you work with kids and then come home to one?"

"Just be patient."

With each conversation, Ciara felt more discouraged than ever before. In her mind, she concluded that her family was not the support she needed. She decided to avoid conversations about herself, her feelings, and her life and maybe avoid her family entirely.

To make matters worse, Ciara frequently spent time browsing social media and following other working moms who appeared to be living very happy, lavish lives, and she wanted that for herself. She noticed how the mothers on social media never looked as exhausted as she felt. They never seemed to struggle financially the way she did. They always posted fancy dinners from upscale restaurants and five-star hotels with beautiful views. Ciara never realized that the posts were mere glimpses of their lives, one-second flashes of their days. She never considered that everything is not what it appears to be and that the people she followed on social media were real people living average lives just like hers. She envied them, never realizing that they were just like her. This unhealthy habit, paired with the unhelpful comments from her family, made Ciara feel low. She became sad most days but didn't know why she felt that way. Although she decided to isolate herself from her family, Ciara was an extrovert at heart and still wanted to find a solution. She turned to friends.

Jamie was one of Ciara's closest friends. They met during their first year of undergrad, shared an English class, and remained friends ever since. Jamie often had similar issues, so venting to Jamie felt like a breath of fresh air to Ciara. The two would exchange stories and share laughs and tears, depending on the subject. They were two peas in a pod, and neither knew how to get out of the ruts they were stuck in. Together, Jamie and Ciara would think of get-rich-quick schemes because they thought money was the answer to their problems. They talked about new businesses they could start. They imagined they would be the dynamic duo and life would turn itself around. They pictured themselves living lavishly and posting on social media from rooftops, wearing couture dresses, fur coats, or skimpy bathing suits and writing catchy captions for all to see. But because Jamie was more of a talker than a doer, those dreams and hopes diminished just as quickly as those conversations ended. Ciara's time with Jamie was great, but nothing fruitful resulted from their dreamy business adventure conversations.

Ciara's search for balance and a life that didn't overwhelm her continued. She began to feel that she had tried everything, as if nothing would work and that giving up was the only other option.

Can you relate to Ciara? Does she remind you of anyone in your life? Does she remind you of yourself? If so, it's because this story is very common. Many people are experiencing what Ciara experienced with her family and close friend. I am here to tell you that giving up is not the answer, and I am also here to show you how I managed to break through this barrier myself.

The problem for Ciara was that she tried everything she and her circle of family and friends could think of. Still, it was limited to their beliefs, experiences, and opinions. There was no shortage of opinions, but certainly, there was more for Ciara to explore.

It is not wrong to feel discouraged after a few failed attempts. However, the solution to your problem may not be found within the first few brainstorming sessions, and it may not exist within your bubble of friends as they have often had similar experiences. Or maybe they have had entirely different experiences that somehow yielded the same unsuccessful results. I invite you all to open your minds, remove any negative self-talk, and accept that there is a world outside of your current circle of friends and their circles of friends. Most times, the answers you may be searching for may be on a road you have yet to travel.

If you're feeling stressed, anxious, or overwhelmed and find that what you have tried in the past has not worked, surely there is someone in this great, big universe who can offer another way. And let's be clear, by "has not worked," I mean the issue is currently causing pain or bringing you unnecessary stress, heartache, or unpleasant feelings. When problems reach this level, even after you've tried so much to resolve them, it's safe to say your resolution tactics are not working. If this is true for you, this chapter is for you. Knowing what your barriers are will allow you to focus on new ways of breaking them. We all know what works for one person may not work for another. We each must find what works for us.

In Ciara's case, although she has a big family, she still feels she doesn't have the support she needs. Most of her family was extremely opinionated and offered unwanted advice, which only worsened Ciara's situation. We all know family and friends who are just like them. Like many people, Ciara focused too much of her time and attention on social media. Her perception of the people she followed was unrealistic. Although she was fun and relatable, Ciara's close friend was a bit of a procrastinator. Ciara didn't realize that repeatedly discussing new business ideas with someone lacking the same level of passion, drive, or interest inadvertently contributed to her feelings of stagnation.

1. **Have hard conversations.**
   Rather than isolating herself from her family, Ciara could have had individual conversations with each person, letting them know that their opinions or advice was not what she needed at the time. She could have told her sister that discussions between them should be kept private and not shared with the entire family.

   We all have had to set boundaries and have had hard conversations in the past. It's never fun, but it can save the relationship and minimize feelings of isolation. It is also a good idea to learn from these types of experiences. If you have a family member or a friend who tells everybody everything, it is a good idea not to let that person be the person with whom you share all your deep, dark secrets. It doesn't need to be an all-or-nothing approach. Just share certain information or parts of your life with that person and then have a go-to person for the more sensitive information.

If individual conversations sound like way too much work, scheduling a time to meet with everyone at once is also an option. It is important to let the people in your life know what you need from them and what you don't need. It is totally fine to be gentle yet firm about your needs. Without having difficult conversations, people are likely to continue unwanted behaviors that they may not know are as bothersome as they are, which will only push you away, driving a wedge between you and the person.

2. **Customize social media experiences and be mindful of your time.** Ciara often feels sad or depressed while scrolling through social media, so minimizing her time on social media or redesigning her social media experience could help her tremendously. As a habit, Ciara would pick up her phone and immediately begin scrolling to see what her friends were posting each day. Even though she often felt sad or envious afterward, she never stopped scrolling.

Did you know you can curate your social media experience to your liking? For those accounts that make you feel sad, angry, irritated, envious, or any other negative feeling, the easy solution is to snooze, delete, or unfollow those accounts. You may want to dig to discover why certain things or people bother you but start with eliminating that negative energy. You don't need it in your life. Instead, think of what makes you happy. What types of accounts inspire you? Begin following and engaging with more of those accounts.

If you are one of the many people who compare your life to the one-second snapshots of others, then consider being gentler with yourself. It is unrealistic to believe that a photo of a person fully captures that person's life and assume that their life must be better than yours. Give yourself grace. Know that no one is perfect, including the people on social media who appear to be.

If you have difficulty with this, consider limiting the time you allow yourself to scroll daily. If you don't currently set time limits and you find yourself scrolling for hours at a time, I hate to be the bearer of bad news, but that could be why you are finding it hard to watch other people live the life you may think you want. Sorry, but someone had to say it. Consider reallocating that time to being productive, such as goal setting, picking up a hobby, or practicing self-care.

3. **Raise your self-awareness and start habit tracking.**
If Ciara had been more aware of the bad habits she had, there is a chance that she would not have spent as much time being sad and miserable or feeling hopeless for as long as she did. She could have realized much sooner that she had some habits that could use a little revamping, and she could have started building new, more beneficial habits. The excellent news for Ciara, and you, if this applies, is that there is always time to begin working on yourself.

We don't always realize that, at times, we cause our own pain and suffering. We all have habits. Some are good, and others not so much. If you find yourself doing things that make you sad, consider not doing those things. Track and write your habits so you become more aware of them. If you need help with this, I have included habit trackers in the *Self-care: A Better Version of Me Workbook*. While you do not need the workbook to get value from this book, it was designed to help readers become more aware of their habits.

Notes

Notes

Chapter 5

The Myths of Self-care

Y ou may have heard some of the common myths about self-care and may believe them to be true. Before we learn how to practice self-care, let's explore some of these myths so that if you consciously or unconsciously believe any of them, you can reframe, get to know a different perspective, and be more open to understanding self-care and all it entails. Some people don't understand that by taking care of yourself, you can better care for everyone else.

Let's dive into this and some of the other myths related to self-care.

Myth #1: Self-care is selfish.
No. No, it's not. Self-care is NOT selfish. There are five reasons one may believe that self-care is selfish: cultural beliefs, misinterpretation, stigma, a lack of understanding, and personal experiences. Let's get into a little more detail.

Cultural Beliefs
Some cultures prioritize self-sacrifice and putting the needs of others before your own, which can lead some people to feel guilty when they prioritize themselves.

Misinterpretation
Some people believe self-care means overindulging, greed, or pampering oneself. They may not realize the full extent of what self-care could look like, how it varies from person to person, and that maintaining mental, physical, and emotional health are forms of self-care.

<u>Stigma</u>

In society, there is a stigma associated with many topics, with well-being and mental health being at the top of the list. Because of the stigma, there is often guilt attached to prioritizing self-care, especially when it conflicts with other roles and responsibilities.

<u>Lack of Understanding</u>

Some people need help understanding the concept of self-care and its importance.

<u>Personal Experiences</u>

Poor past experiences or messaging from other people may cause a person to avoid practicing self-care, especially if they were previously criticized, judged, or neglected.

What we will learn in future chapters is that self-care is not selfish; rather, it's a necessity. It benefits the person who is practicing, but it also benefits everyone in that person's care as well.

Myth #2: Self-care is time-consuming.
Here is where I challenge everyone who
doesn't practice self-care simply because they
feel they don't have time. In a later chapter,
I will explain exactly how to create time for
self-care even if it feels like you don't have
any, but for now, let's briefly discuss the
time it can take for a small act of self-care.

Going for a walk takes as long as you allow.
You could set a timer and walk five minutes
away from home, then walk five minutes
back. That wouldn't be considered a lot of
exercise, but that time could be used to clear
your mind, make a quick phone call, or get
some fresh air.

Taking five minutes to sit and enjoy a cup of
coffee instead of drinking it on the go is
another example of achieving self-care in a
short time. Other examples include reading,
journaling, or listening to your favorite song.
In Chapter 8, we will cover over 100 ways to
practice self-care. Sure, there are more time-
consuming acts of self-care, but there are
many ways that can take less than 30

minutes, some less than 20 minutes. And honestly, if you care for others for hours each day, either at work or home, you deserve 20 minutes for yourself. Just remember, something is better than nothing when it comes to loving and caring for yourself.

Myth #3: Self-care costs too much.
This is only true if you've been misinformed or you misunderstand the meaning of self-care. If you imagine self-care to only consist of being on a luxury yacht, flying first class overseas, and taking weeklong vacations, then yes, for many people, self-care costs entirely too much. If this were the only form of self-care, some people would never experience what self-care feels like in their lifetime. Luckily, I have news for you. There is so much more to self-care than these lavish ideas.

Sometimes, it isn't about what you buy yourself and how much it costs; it's more about what you do with your time. If you are a coffee or tea drinker and you make your drink at home daily, going to a coffee shop for 20-30 minutes can be your self-care for the day. Spending a few bucks on a coffee and allowing yourself to sit quietly, electronic-free, so you can fully focus on being present at that moment can feel like more than enough for someone with young children at home whose coffee is usually cold before they finish drinking it. It's the simple things.

You could sit silently in a library or at a park, which are both free. In moments of silence, we gain clarity. Can you imagine the busyness of the mind of someone who never experiences calmness and quiet? Noise becomes the norm. Getting a moment to sit still may be a challenge for the person who is always on the go. But sitting, purposely, to gather your thoughts or meditate for just 15 minutes can be self-care.

Yes, some forms of self-care cost money, and they can range from free to thousands of dollars, but there are also cheap or free ways to practice -self-care. Regardless of which form you choose or how much money or time you choose to invest, it is important not to skip self-care altogether due to a lack of time or funds.

Myth #4: Self-care is only for people who are stressed.
This myth reminds me of the old movies where a person would have a psychotic episode ending up in a recovery facility where they would address their mental health concerns. While those movies are real life for many people, I urge everyone not to wait until they have reached a breaking point to realize we all need and benefit from self-care.

Stress can indeed cause more damage than one could ever imagine. The key is to take care of our mental, emotional, and physical well-being regularly, regardless of whether we have severe concerns. Everyone has a breaking point. Some of our thresholds are higher than others. Self-care allows us to reduce the chances of experiencing such breaks.

Myth #5: Self-care is only about pampering yourself.

We've covered this topic a little, but since it's such a popular thought, I decided to have it as its own myth, too. While visiting a spa, taking a warm bath surrounded by candles, and getting a massage can be aspects of a particular type of self-care, they do not fully encompass all there is to practicing self-care. The purpose of the spa, bubble bath, or massage is to promote relaxation, rejuvenation, and overall well-being. However, there are hundreds of other ways to achieve the same results.

When we think about self-care, it is vital to think about it holistically, focusing on physical self-care, emotional self-care, and mental self-care. Physical self-care includes getting enough sleep, eating healthily, attending to your hygiene, and exercising. Emotional self-care includes setting boundaries, practicing self-compassion and positive self-talk, expressing emotions, and knowing when and how to seek support, to name a few. Mental self-care includes mindfulness, engaging in hobbies and interests, challenging negative thoughts, and much more.

Self-care is much more than pampering. It's about holistically nurturing and caring for oneself, maintaining balance, resilience, and well-being. It's prioritizing life in such a way that you feel recharged so that you can handle life, its challenges, and everything it throws your way without running out of steam, and that looks different for all of us.

Myth #6: People who practice self-care are rude/mean.
Is this a myth or a misconception? Either way, it is not a fact. Some people are not kind, but I like to believe that most people in this world are good people. The problem comes when we cannot distinguish the good from the bad, so we overgeneralize, and everyone gets placed into the same category. For anyone who believes this myth to be true, I challenge you to try different

experiences. You would be doing yourself a disservice to continue assuming that everyone fits into one bucket.

Myth #7: Self-care is revenge.
We are not being nice to ourselves to get back at someone for something they did. Self-care is about you; the focus should be on you. It is not about letting the other person see or think you have a good life. It is about genuinely finding and experiencing the good in life. Retaliation is not the goal, ever.

Myth #8: Self-care is for people who deserve it, not me.
Sometimes, we are hard on ourselves and can be our worst critics. The reality is that everyone needs a few days, hours, or even minutes to rest, recharge, and reset. The thought that you must continually prove yourself to others or that others are more worthy than you is unhealthy and self-destructive. Everyone deserves self-care.

Myth #9: Self-care is not necessary.
This myth is common among hard-working, high-achieving individuals. This person's schedule is busy every day, and they are constantly on the go from morning until night. They may not see a need for me-time and find taking a break of any kind to be unimportant and unnecessary. It could be that they find it time-consuming. Still, other times, they think it is optional to do things for themselves and may not see time available in their busy schedules, so they skip it.

If the previous paragraph describes you or your life, please know you must create time to be self-nurtured. From personal experience, I can assure you that self-care is definitely for you. If you don't make the time, the consequences may present themselves in the worst ways at the worst times. When you take time for yourself, you will likely realize that self-care is one of the best things to happen to you.

Sometimes, we believe myths without knowing they are myths. We reviewed nine myths related to self-care. You may find or know of other myths as well. Here is a list of the myths we covered.

<u>Common Myths</u>

- Self-care is selfish.
- Self-care is time-consuming.
- Self-care costs too much.
- Self-care is only for people who are stressed.
- Self-care is only about pampering yourself.
- People who practice self-care are rude/mean.
- Self-care is revenge.
- Self-care is for people who deserve it, not me.
- Self-care is not necessary.

Notes

Notes

Chapter 6

The Breakthrough

Now that we've defined self-care and burnout, discovered various barriers, explained the importance of self-discovery, and we've even debunked common myths, it's time to get to the good part; the breakthrough! To truly live your best life and be your best version of yourself, you need to understand exactly how much you mean to the world. Okay, that might be a stretch because quite honestly, we don't often see the impact a person has on the world until after their passing, and even more unfortunate than that, there are people who never recognize their own greatness. Let's rephrase. To truly become the best version of you, it is essential to take care of yourself.

Regardless of what led you to decide to become a better version of yourself, the wonderful news is the fact that you have arrived. The breakthrough comes when you say enough is enough. No longer will I put myself last on the to-do list, no more will I do for others without doing for myself and gone are the days when I don't matter. Simply put, I am significant, and I will behave as such.

And no, you are not being selfish.

We are breaking free from people, places, and things that don't serve us. We are going to set boundaries, and we are going to adhere to those boundaries. We are also going to ensure others understand and respect our boundaries as well. We will stop people-pleasing. We will no longer lose ourselves, while trying to make everyone else happy, placing our own happiness on the back burner.

Earlier on, I mentioned how I overworked myself straight into depression, how my doctor scolded me for thinking I should feel 'normal', whatever that means, and how life was rough for me. When I left that office and proceeded to cry my heart out, I began to break through.

I broke through the idea that my children needed to be in multiple extracurricular activities. I let go of whatever it was that made me feel guilty about not signing up for another ballet lesson and another swim lesson. At work, I had somewhat of a choice as to which families I would work with and which ones just drained too much of my energy. I began to exercise that right to choose. I began to say no. For the first time in a long time, I said no. That was a pivotal time for me.

Things didn't get better instantly. I would love to say I became superwoman, and every day around 5:30 p.m., I whipped out my cape and turned into Super Toya, but it didn't quite happen that way. In fact, it took a long time, a very long time for me to overcome what I was going through. Did I mention that in the months leading up to the doctor's visit, I worked seven days each week? During the week, I worked with the children and families, and on the weekends, I bartended at a local chain restaurant. For six months straight, I worked for seven days every week, taking no days off. And I wondered why I was depressed. All that I was doing was a recipe for disaster. I couldn't see it, but I ended up right on Disaster Avenue.

It's funny how humans think. I mean, I was killing myself, both mentally and physically, and I was expecting just to be okay with it. This just shows how hard we can be on ourselves. I believe most of us are our own worst critics. Let's normalize being easier on ourselves and giving ourselves the same grace we give to others.

For me, I was at a point where I knew something needed to change, and that change needed to happen expeditiously. My health depended on it. So, what did I do? I'm glad you asked.

I took ownership and accountability for my actions and realized I was the reason I was in this huge mess. I could blame people in my life at the time or people from my past, but at the end of the day, I was my own barrier. I needed a breakthrough.

My mom gave me the simplest advice. She told me to start treating myself and taking care of myself regularly. She mentioned that it could be something as simple as going out for a cup of my favorite coffee instead of making it at home. And so, I did. Thanks, Mom!

It wasn't easy at first, but I kept one thing in mind: the need to take better care of myself. I began to think more about what I needed, my health, my lifestyle, and changes that needed to be made. I quit my second job. I skipped the ballet signup. I even skipped swimming. In the most unselfish way, I adopted a me-first mentality.

Key Takeaways

- After discovering your barriers, if you want change, you must do something different. Use the knowledge you've gained to begin breaking free from limiting factors.

- Breaking free involves intentionality. It also involves battling unhealthy belief systems, thought patterns, and people. It may be challenging, but when you begin to make yourself a priority, and you begin to see what that feels like, it will definitely be worth it.

Notes

Notes

Chapter 7

Adopting a

"Me-First" Mentality

I found it extremely difficult to begin putting myself first. For five years, my maternal instincts had led me to put my children first, so I knew I had my work cut out for me. It wasn't that I didn't have the time for myself. Time was certainly hard to find, but that wasn't the real problem. The real problem was that I had gotten so lost in my children, their health and well-being, their education, and their little lives that I forgot about my own.

I took my parenting role extremely seriously. I was Toya, the mom, and aside from the few and far between times when I would conjure up enough energy to get dressed and hang out with friends for a couple of hours, which were challenging times to enjoy and fully engage because even in those moments, I still thought of my children. I was dedicated to my children, their activities, and whatever they were involved in at the moment. I made excuses for not focusing on myself. Some of them were valid, such as the fact that finding good childcare was, and still is, expensive and quite difficult. Pair that with the inconvenience of packing bags for the children if it was a drop-off babysitter or preparing meals, setting out pajamas, and praying the kids would behave while I was gone if the sitter was coming to us. It really was a lot of work for the amount of time I would be gone. Oftentimes, I opted out. The thought of it all was more than I could handle. The funny thing is, I always had it at the back of my mind that I needed help, but somehow it never made it to my priority list, and that felt normal.

What I later realized was that I didn't know what self-care looked like. It could have slapped me in the face, and I wouldn't have been able to recognize it because it was so foreign to me. I needed to find myself. I was no longer the person I once was prior to having children. I needed a breakthrough from the person I had become; the one who didn't focus on me. So, what was I to do?

My first step in adopting a me-first attitude in the most loving and unselfish way was to consciously begin breaking habits that pushed me to the background unconsciously. Breaking any habit can be hard to do, but once you become intentional, it becomes much easier over time. When we develop norms due to our subconscious mindset, those norms become second nature and we do them without thinking and without assessing their importance, relevance, or necessity. For many people and even some animals, family is their most valued possession. I wholeheartedly understand this way of thinking. However, always putting your family and responsibilities first before caring for your own needs may not always be the wisest decision. Simply put, you cannot pour into others if there is nothing left in your cup. You must fill your own cup and continuously fill your cup so that you can pour generously into others.

If you ever want to make big changes, start small. Attempting to start anything by taking too big of a step will likely result in failure. I decided to start with my shopping habits. Previously, whenever I went to clothing stores, the norm was to head straight to the children's section. But guess who needed new tops and bottoms? I will give you a hint. It was not the children. The problem was that I had programmed myself to think *only* of my children. When I went grocery shopping, I picked up foods *the kids would like.* I noticed this was a habit and had become my way of thinking everywhere I went and with everything I did.

To reclaim my sense of self-worth and my own identity, I had to go into stores with serious intentions. I began to talk to myself, not aloud, but silently and I would tell myself to stay focused. I would say, "If I am the one who needs clothes, I need to go to the adult section and avoid the children's section." It was not easy. To be honest, it is now a decade later, and it still isn't easy to avoid the children's section. In my defense, I have added one more child to the bunch and now have another reason to visit the children's section. Let's say it's a work in progress. Practice makes perfect, they say. So, here's to more practice.

Another habit that took me ages to learn was this one: LEARNING TO SAY NO.

Why Saying "No" is Important

The word no sets boundaries. It's a simple, easy word, one of the first words a toddler learns and holds onto. It's also a word people tend to struggle with due to guilt or fear. Learning to say no is vital to experiencing peace of mind. Overcoming the eager desire to be everything to everyone, to do everything for whoever asks, is the type of self-care we all need.

Saying yes is not such a bad thing, but it should never be at the expense of your own needs: relaxation, time to recover, financial abilities, etc. Being available to people is only worthwhile if you are also sensitive to yourself. You must learn how to be present for yourself first.

No one should ever have to choose between oneself and others. However, people make sacrifices like this daily. At some point in life, most people will be faced with a time when they feel pulled in multiple directions and may need to say no to a coworker, friend, or family member. It may not always be easy to own your time, but no one is expected to be available one hundred percent of the time. Listed below are ways to say no politely but assertively.

1. "No."
2. "Something came up and I will not be able to make it."
3. "I have other plans."
4. "The idea sounds great; however, I'm not qualified for that job."
5. "Thanks so much for believing in me, but I'm sorry I cannot help you this time."
6. "I don't have the time for that right now."
7. "Can I recommend someone else to help you with that?"
8. "I trust that you can handle it perfectly on your own."
9. "Let me think about it. I will get back to you."
10. "I am not the right person for the job."

11. "I do not have the time for that right now, but we can reschedule another time."
12. "I am too exhausted at the moment for that. I need a rest."
13. "I am not comfortable with that."
14. "I need some me-time right now."
15. "It's a no for me."
16. "I am afraid that will not be possible."
17. "I appreciate the offer, but I have to decline."
18. "I have other commitments right now."
19. "I'm committed to another project right now."
20. "I've reached my limit for now."

Remember, saying no is a natural part of setting boundaries and prioritizing your well-being. Choose an approach that aligns with the situation and your communication style.

It can be difficult for a person with no clear boundaries to say no or to let people know when they have crossed their line. Take time to evaluate your relationships carefully. Understand the role you play in said relationships. Recognize that most relationships will survive even if you say no. Sometimes, you will encounter individuals who don't know how to respect your boundaries. Listed below are some ways I recommend dealing with these individuals kindly.

1. "I think you're a great person, but I don't feel like our boundaries align. Thanks for your time."
2. "I have a lot going on in my life right now, and I am not able to prioritize our relationship."
3. "It's been great getting to know you, but I don't think our values align. I hope you understand."
4. "I don't want any further contact with you; please respect my decision."
5. "I have stated my boundaries repeatedly, and I don't think you respect them enough. It's best we stop talking."

It is so much better to address the person using one of the sentences above or create your own instead of ghosting them. It shows you have respect for other people and know how to communicate. Boundary setting can work personally and professionally, too.

In addition to ridding myself of unwanted habits, I also worked to establish new ones. I began to read more. I consider myself a lifelong learner, and I love reading nonfiction. The more I read, the more I learn, and as I learn more and more, I realize how little we all know, even if we think we know a lot. Reading can fill you with so much knowledge that you feel like you have entered a new and amazing world again and again. Reading personal development and self-help books allowed me the opportunity to explore new ways of living, thinking, and being. I started including new practices and routines into my schedule based on what I read, and I enjoyed it; it brought a different kind of fulfillment because, unlike taking care of responsibilities for someone else, I was doing something for myself.

This was how I began to reclaim my time—taking down one barrier at a time. Little by little, I started feeling like my old self again. I felt loved and lovable. My kids loved the version of me that wasn't always tired at night. Of course, this version was more fun. My body felt a lot lighter, and for the first time in a while, I was practicing self-care. I learned that embarking on a journey of self-care involves understanding that self-care isn't selfish. If you don't understand that, you may find yourself procrastinating, making excuses, and prioritizing everything and everyone else.

- Reclaiming your time involves finally taking note of the fact that you are a part of the equation of your life and that self-care is not selfish.

- Sometimes, you need to say "No," and that is okay.

- Evaluating your habits is important. Changing poor habits and adding new habits is how we grow.

Notes

Notes

Chapter 8

What can Self-care Look Like?

There are many ideas about self-care and what it looks and feels like, and the truth is that it can look and feel differently for each individual. Self-care is often referred to as a journey because we need to care for ourselves regularly, it takes time to get it right, and we are never truly finished. It isn't something you do once and never need to do again. It's ongoing. Sometimes we fall off track, but the beauty of the journey is that we can always hop back on and begin again.

Self-care ideas can range from cheap or free to expensive and outrageous. Guess what? Both are okay. I'd advise you to stay within your budget. There are plenty of events, acts of self-care, and other things to do that can be done with limited to no budget at all, so please do not be discouraged and do not focus on what you cannot do. Remember, the focus is self-care, which requires being gentle and kind to yourself.

I've created a comprehensive list of self-care activities. As you read this list, take note of which activities interest you the most.

1. Exercise.
2. Keep a diary.
3. Start journaling.
4. Take an extra-long shower, purposely.
5. Practice mindfulness.
6. Begin a new skincare routine.
7. Take a nap.
8. Try a new recipe.

9. Order food for takeout.
10. Have a picnic.
11. Go for a walk.
12. Pray.
13. Do yoga.
14. Find a new exercise video.
15. Take it back to your childhood roots and color a picture.
16. Paint.
17. Draw a picture.
18. Join an online community that interests you.
19. Host an event with a few of your friends.
20. Contact an old friend.
21. Write an email to your favorite author or someone who has inspired you.
22. Read a new book.
23. Read an old one.
24. Visit a museum.
25. Visit the zoo.
26. Visit your local park.
27. Listen to soothing music.
28. Listen to your favorite song.
29. Dance like no one is watching.
30. Give yourself permission to binge-watch a show.
31. Do a craft.

32. Start and finish a Do-It-Yourself (DIY) project.
33. Organize an area of your home.
34. Listen to your favorite song and dance like nobody's watching.
35. Take a mental health day.
36. Use an oil diffuser.
37. Burn a candle.
38. Watch one of your favorite movies.
39. Pick up a new hobby.
40. Go for a drive.
41. Stretch.
42. Plan a vacation.
43. Get dressed up for no good reason.
44. Listen to a podcast.
45. Make your favorite dessert.
46. Declutter.
47. Watch the sunrise or sunset.
48. Unplug.
49. Get an hour of extra sleep.
50. Learn how to do something new.
51. Take an online course.
52. Treat yourself to something special.
53. Get a massage.
54. Write a list of 5 reasons you are grateful.
55. Break from your norm in some way.
56. Learn to sew, quilt, or crochet.
57. Write a poem.

58. Write a random thank you letter.
59. Try learning a new language.
60. Skip checking emails for a day.
61. Read a magazine.
62. Visit a library or bookstore.
63. Do a puzzle.
64. Listen to an audiobook.
65. Practice positive self-talk.
66. Do something that makes you happy.
67. Have a Positivity Day! Speak no negative words.
68. Write 5 amazing things about yourself.
69. Practice meditation.
70. Write 5 positive affirmations.
71. Make a vision board.
72. Make a photo album, either online or a physical book.
73. Create a collage.
74. Write a book.
75. Start a collection.
76. Write a note to your future self.
77. Give to a charity or a cause.
78. Surprise someone with a small gift. (extra tip)
79. Choose a day to be gentle to yourself. Only speak kind words. You've probably been your harshest critic for years.
80. Write for 5 minutes without stopping.

81. Go for a bike ride.
82. Go hiking.
83. Go camping.
84. Go to a sporting event.
85. Go to a fancy hotel for a night. Order room service. Relax and unwind.
86. Buy flowers for yourself or as a gift.
87. Go underclothes shopping.
88. Watch a comedy.
89. Splurge (within reason).
90. Go to a wine tasting or make your own.
91. Hire a housecleaner just this once.
92. Write a letter to the old version of yourself. Apologize if you need to.
93. Create a playlist.
94. Sit in silence.
95. Ask for help.
96. Watch the company you keep.
97. Search for inspiration. Look outside of your comfort zone.
98. Pay it forward.
99. Smile at someone.
100. Compliment someone.
101. Take a day trip.
102. Relax.
103. Give to someone less fortunate.
104. Be gentle with your expectations of yourself and others.

105. Rearrange your space to create a more peaceful environment.
106. Make a list of all the things you love.
107. Make a list of goals.
108. Go on a date alone.

Hopefully, you enjoyed this list of self-care ideas and found some of them interesting enough to add to your personal list. Now, let's take time to review each of them to gain a better understanding of why and how each activity can add value to your life. You might want to grab a snack and put your feet up as you dive into this list.

1. **Exercise.** This is one of the most common, and most well-known forms of self-care. The benefits of exercise are plentiful, and there is no doubt that being physically active can work wonders for the mind, body, and soul. Here are just five of the many benefits of exercising.

   According to the Center for Disease Control and Prevention (CDC), exercise:

   • Helps to control your weight.
   • Helps to improve mental health.

- Strengthens bones and muscles.
- Reduces risks of some illnesses.
- Increases the chance of living longer.

2. **Keep a diary.** Diary is a bit of an old term that describes what most refer to as journaling nowadays. Diaries seemed to be a little more personal; a place to hide your deep dark secrets with the expectations of no one ever reading them. Many diaries came with locks that needed a teeny-tiny key to open them. In addition to the diary being a place to write your thoughts, it also provided a sense of secrecy, privacy, or ownership.

3. **Journaling.** Journaling has been around for quite some time, but we can kind of look at it as the new age diary to some extent. Much like keeping a diary, journaling provides a place to unload your thoughts, and it is very popular these days amongst all age groups from grade school children and teens to midlife and older individuals, too.

Journaling is the practice of writing or recording your feelings, thoughts, or experiences. Your journaling process can be as simple or complex as you allow it to be. There are stickers specifically made and sold for people who do journal writing. Some people have schedules of when to write. For example, there are people who write every morning before getting out of bed as a way of getting started with the day. Then, there are those who prefer to write before bed as a way of clearing their minds to help them to sleep better.

There are those who choose traditional methods of journal writing and will use pen and paper. Then, there are those who use colorful markers, die cut stickers, daily themes, and all the bells and whistles. More recently, there is a new wave of journal writers who don't actually write at all. These people use an online word processor or an audio or video recorder. Regardless of the method, the benefits are almost all the same.

Mental health benefits of journaling include the following:

- Journaling helps the brain to identify, analyze, and regulate emotions.
- Journaling assists with prioritizing fears, problems, and moods.
- Journaling can help a person to sleep better, especially if they make a routine of writing at night.
- Journaling can be a tool for communicating more effectively.

There are many more benefits to journaling than what is included here, so if you are considering journaling, this may be a great option for you. Some people find writing their thoughts or reflecting on their days to be cathartic, relaxing, and stress-relieving. It can feel therapeutic to bring clarity to your thoughts, setting goals and tracking them, or being artistic and creative.

4.   **Take an extra-long shower.** Showering is a great way to practice self-care regularly and affordably. Of course, we all

need to clean ourselves. But often, we speed through the process, spending just enough time to cleanse our faces, bodies, and maybe our hair. Then, we rush off to the next task on the to-do list.

Intentionally taking more time than necessary in the shower can:

- Relieve stress.
- Allow a person time to refocus.
- Offer a much-needed moment of privacy.
- Provide relaxation during a stressful time.
- Wash off germs and help prevent illnesses.

If you're shower time is so routine and robotic that you are wondering what you would do with extra time in the shower, consider the following options:

- Give yourself a second or third cleansing.
- Stand still in the shower, allowing the water to run down your back.

- Take the time to be in the moment.
- Listen to music or an audiobook.
- Practice deep breathing.
- Begin a new skin or foot care routine.

5. **Practice mindfulness.** Two words - mindfulness matters. To practice mindfulness is to be alert, paying close attention to the present moment. Let's take a moment to practice mindfulness right now.

First, follow these three steps. One, relax your shoulders. Two, unclench your jaw. Three, lower your tongue from the roof of your mouth. How did I do? Was I three for three? We often move in certain ways without paying any attention to what we are doing or how we are doing it.

For example, unless there is a delicious smell coming from the oven or a really stinky smell coming from the trash, we don't always pay attention to the smells around us. The same is true for what we feel. When was the last time you paid attention to the ground underneath your feet? We are simply too busy running and keeping up with work demands and what everyone else is doing to sit, or stand, and pay attention to ourselves in a mindful way.

There is no right or wrong way to practice mindfulness. One person may choose to go out into nature to listen to the crickets and the sounds of birds and other animals or creatures. Another person may meditate in their bedroom. One person may practice box breathing or another breathing technique, while someone else listens to a guided meditation video.

The purpose of practicing mindfulness is to stop thinking about the past or the future and to live in the current moment free from distractions. This practice is known to reduce stress, improve mental and emotional health, and increase focus and concentration. These are just a few of the benefits of practicing mindfulness.

6. **Begin a new skincare routine.** Taking care of our physical health and hygiene is practicing self-care as well. I would like to group a few self-care tips into this one. Focusing on skincare could include getting a facial, trying a new face mask, buying a new face cream or cleanser, making your own face cream or cleanser, and many more ideas. Just taking time to care for your skin in a way that you don't currently do can help you gain a new sense of self-worth and self-confidence. If you have no idea where to start, there are books, magazines, videos, and even podcasts that do a wonderful job of explaining various products, their benefits, and some even compare different products, which can be helpful to get an idea of what may interest you.

7. **Take a nap.** This is one of the best, most rejuvenating forms of self-care. Naps can

work wonders. They can change your mood, reset your day, and make you feel brand new. Don't underestimate the power of a nap. However, if you have trouble sleeping at night, I do not recommend taking a nap during the day. The results of that could end unfavorably.

Most adults don't need a ton of convincing to take a nap, but if you're interested in learning more about how a nap can benefit you, here's a short list. Naps can:

- Improve your ability to stay alert.
- Help to deal with frustration and irritability.
- Improve memory.
- Reduce fatigue.
- Help to increase performance.
- Make you feel super charged and ready for the day.

8. **Try a new recipe**. Regardless of our diets, most of us have the same recipes that we put on rotation and rarely deviate from the list. Think of a dish that you love,

but don't often make yourself. Try to put your own spin on it, or maybe try to duplicate it exactly the way you remember having it. Just remember to be gentle with yourself if it doesn't turn out exactly as expected.

Trying something new can be adventurous. Best case, you love it and have a new recipe to add to the rotation. Worst case, you learn that the recipe you thought would be delicious actually was not, and you can try to something different the next time.

Here are a few reasons to try a new recipe:

- Expand your options.
- Tempt your taste buds.
- Travel to a new country by creating their foods in your own kitchen.
- Be creative.
- Make mealtime exciting.

9.   **Order takeout**. If you're tired of cooking and need a little break, consider picking up takeout or ordering delivery. Everyone deserves a break. Takeout usually makes everyone happy and saves so much time in the kitchen. It can be a little costly with delivery fees, service fees, taxes, and all the other random fees. I cannot pretend like it's cheap, but every now and then, it's nice to be able to skip the dishes. Having fewer dishes is always a win!

10. **Have a picnic.** The best part about this idea is you can either go with someone or go alone. Being in your own company can be enjoyable. It's a good time to self-reflect, listen to music, breathe, practice journaling, or just be in the moment. Another bonus is it's much cheaper.

If the thought of dining alone scares you or makes you feel weird, it may be time to get a little more comfortable with yourself. Too often, we depend on other people to have fun and enjoy life. It might be time to get used to the idea of not allowing people or their absence to deprive you of experiences. Being alone is different from being lonely. The reality is if you cannot enjoy your own company, how can you expect someone else to enjoy it?

11. **Go for a walk.** For those of us with God given abilities to walk, we often take it for granted. Some of us even complain when we need to walk farther than we'd like. As I sit here typing with a sprained ankle, I've been reminded how fortunate we are and how grateful we need to be. Walk provides a host of benefits physically, mentally, and overall.

Did you know that walking does all of the following?

- Reduces the risk of heart disease.
- Improves heart health.
- Helps with controlling, maintaining, and losing weight.
- Enhances blood circulation.

- Helps to maintain a healthy blood pressure.
- Contributes to better sleeping.
- Promotes muscle strength.
- Improves joint flexibility.
- Reduces stiffness.
- Alleviates bloating and digestion issues.
- Boosts energy levels.
- Burns calories.
- Can be a social activity preventing feelings of isolation.
- Reduces the risk of chronic diseases.
- Improves mood.
- And so much more!

In addition to the endless benefits associated with walking, there are also many options and ways to incorporate walking into your regular routine. You could walk alone, with someone, start a walking group, or go with your pet if you have one. You could speedwalk or go at a snail's pace. It really doesn't matter. With so many good reasons to walk, the question is why wouldn't you?

12. **Pray.** If you believe in the power of
     prayer, and even if you struggle in this
     area, you may find that taking time to
     speak to God or whatever higher power
     you believe in can bring a sense of peace
     and comfort.

     Prayer can reduce stress causing
     individuals to feel a sense of calm and
     inner peace. Prayer is often a time to
     express gratitude, seek guidance, and
     hope for positive life changes. When a
     person prays, they have a conversation
     with God on a personal level. In those
     moments, no one is there to judge the
     person or the conversation. They are free
     to speak as freely as they wish. Some
     people take this time to seek forgiveness,
     express their intent to improve, or simply
     say thank you.

13. **Do yoga.** Yoga is another popular form of
     self-care. It combines breathing exercises,
     body exercises, and simple meditation and
     can be very relaxing. There are many

different types of yoga, all with different levels of difficulty.

Yoga is known to enhance flexibility, build muscle strength, and improve posture. However, yoga is much more than just physical exercise. It focuses on the mind and body simultaneously. Mindful breathing and meditation, which are often a part of yoga, help to reduce stress and promote relaxation. If you are interested in trying yoga, I suggest researching the benefits.

14. **Find a new exercise video.** Perhaps you currently have an exercise routine but want to try something new. Maybe you have a friend who also wants to try a new exercise routine. This could be an opportunity to deviate from the norm a little bit. You would still get your workout, just with a little twist. You never know. You might actually enjoy the new workout and want to incorporate some parts of it into your daily or weekly routine.

Finding an exercise video that you love can be challenging, but exploring different options can be the key to ending inactivity. Luckily, there are beginner-friendly videos for newbies or people who want to keep it light, and then there are high-intensity workout videos for more experienced people who want to burn more calories.

15. **Color a picture.** Take it back to your childhood days and find a picture you'd like to color. There are adult coloring books with intricate designs if you really want to take this idea to the next level. Coloring a child's coloring book can be just as relaxing, so don't worry yourself if you don't have an adult coloring book.

Whenever I color with children as a creative activity, I find myself being the last one at the table. While the kids typically have a short attention span for art, I tend to get lost in the colors and can

sit for hours creating my version of a
masterpiece.

In addition to being a creative outlet, art
is also cathartic; it's a way to process and
cope with emotions, trauma, or
challenging experiences. In some ways, it's
a temporary escape from one world to
another. Engaging in art activities can
enhance one's ability to focus and
concentrate. Art is a form of expression,
but did you know it is also a form of
communication?

16. **Paint.** Painting is said to be therapeutic
     because it allows the painter to focus
     solely on the current image. Art is used in
     therapy as a stress reducer and a source of
     relaxation. Painting can be very
     inexpensive. However, the more you
     explore, the more costly it can become.

17. **Draw a picture.** Much like coloring and
     painting, drawing can be just as relaxing.

Allow your mind to take over as the pen touches the paper. If you have no idea what to draw, start with shapes, a house, or an animal. The purpose of this self-care activity is less about being a proud artist and more about taking time to do something for yourself. While you are drawing, you are allowing your mind to relax, calm down, and focus.

18. **Join an online community that interests you.** Nowadays, almost everything you want or need is online and finding a group of people who like to do what you like to do is easier than ever before. If you like rock climbing, real estate, sky diving, or cooking, guess what? There are communities of people who also like those activities. There is nothing like finding your people, not your family or friends, I mean those people who are completely unrelated to you and don't know you, yet you all have this one thing in common that makes it super exciting to exchange stories and engage in discussions. Those are your people!

Some online communities allow people to network, share information or advice, and ask questions. Others offer users the opportunity to collaborate or support one another as they face similar experiences. For example, parenting groups allow parents to meet other parents who may face similar parenting challenges. Doing so allows parents to realize they are not alone and gives them hope that each challenge is just a phase that will pass with time.

19. **Host an event with a few of your friends.** Whether it's a ladies' night, a vision board party, or just a random get-together, meeting up with friends is a great way to restore your energy and have a good time. Don't overthink it. Simple can go a long way when it comes to having friends over. Keep in mind they are coming to see you, not your house, so don't drive yourself insane when it comes to preparing for their arrival.

20. **Contact an old friend.** Reaching out to a friend with whom you may have lost contact can be fun. You'll likely reminisce about good times, catch up on current events, and even plan an event for the future.

21. **Write an email to your favorite author or someone who has inspired you.** My email is authorlatoyadthomas@gmail.com, and I'd be happy to hear from you.

22. **Read a new book.** Reading can be an excellent way to learn new things, calm yourself, relax, and wind down. Some people set reading goals to keep track of how many pages they read per day, per week, or how many books they read each year. Each person's goal is personal to them, and there is no right or wrong number of books to read.

Reading stimulates the mind, increases vocabulary, and provides a mental break from the daily stresses of life. Regular reading also improves a person's writing skills over time. People read for various reasons, but if you haven't heard, reading contributes to a well-rounded, more fulfilling life, so just by reading this book you are on the right track.

23. **Read an old book**. Do you own a book that you haven't read in a long time? Why not reread it? Sometimes rereading a book can make certain parts more interesting. Sometimes when we read, we don't pay full attention to every single detail. Rereading can make every tiny detail make sense in ways that you may not have noticed the first time around. I've read one of my favorite books written by Robert Kiyosaki five times. Each time, something different caught my attention as if I'd completely skipped it the times before that time.

24. **Visit a museum.** Going to a museum as an adult is a different experience than going as a child. If you haven't been to a museum since your elementary school field trips, you may want to consider going to one, two, or a few. As a parent, I recently began going to museums again. To increase visitors on certain days, many museums offer reduced admission for one or two days each. Sometimes, the museums are completely free.

25. **Go to your local zoo.** The zoo can be a fun trip for people of all ages! Not only do you get to see the animals interacting with one another, but you also get a ton of exercise. If you want to increase the number of steps you take, the zoo is the place to go. In my experience, the animals tend to be most active early in the morning during the first hour of the zoo's opening. Going this early almost guarantees a good parking space, as the spaces often fill up quickly.

Planning ahead is essential when traveling to any zoo. You will want to check the zoo's website for their hours of operation, ticket prices, special events, parking information, and discounts. Wear comfortable clothing and shoes. Again, there will be a lot of walking. Don't wear the too-small shoes; the ones that are super cute but hurt your baby toe. You will regret it within the first thirty minutes. Don't forget to take lots of pictures and drink lots of water, too.

26. **Visit your local park.** Even if there is a lot of foot traffic, your local park can be one of the most peaceful places to go. It's a place to go and set your worries aside. For the short time you're there, you can just breathe and enjoy nature. People-watching can be fun, too. However, even the busiest of parks have their quiet times. Take time to enjoy the world around you. Notice the small things like the cracks in the ground, the flowers, murals, cars as they ride by, the sun, the children playing, or the stillness if it's quiet. Think about life, plan, and

strategize your next moves, or simply sit and do nothing at all.

If you plan to stay a while, pack a picnic. Make as big a deal as you'd like or keep it extremely simple. You can take a blanket and spread it out, bring a picnic basket, and listen to some music. You can bring a journal and write or a book to read. It truly is whatever you make it. I've seen very well-thought-out picnics with wine glasses, fresh fruits, and cheeses, and I've seen very simple, easy picnics with a couple of sandwiches, drinks, and a snack. Whatever you decide, enjoy your day at the park. You deserve it!

27. **Listen to soothing music.** The type of music you listen to can influence your mood. Even if soft music isn't your usual, it's a great idea to listen to calming music every now and then. If you have ever been to a spa, you may remember the mindfulness music playing quietly in the background. This was not by accident. The

purpose of this music is to get you to relax and enjoy the moment.

The best part about music is that you can take it anywhere you go. Even on an airplane 35,000 feet into the air, you can listen to music. Interestingly, for some people, when the sound of music is turned off, they can still hear and feel the beat. Did you know that music can help with falling asleep? It can also be a motivator. This is why there are workout playlists for people who need a little inspiration in the gym.

28. **Listen to your favorite song.** Do you have a favorite song? Has it stayed the same for many years? Is your favorite song closely related to a special time in your life? Listening to your favorite song can trigger positive emotions and memories of special moments in life. Your favorite song is like having an old friend who is always there to reminisce and

uplift you. It's a nostalgic feeling to relive the good times.

29. **Dance like nobody's watching.**
Dancing feels good, and dancing to your favorite song is the best feeling. I love this form of self-care because it's effortless and doesn't take a lot of time. Let's face it, not all of us have a ton of free time on our hands. I get it! But we all have three minutes on any given day to play a song and live our best lives while it's playing. Dancing is one of the best forms of physical activity because it doesn't feel like work. It's a great source of cardio and even helps with flexibility.

30. **Give yourself permission to binge-watch a show**. I love this option, mostly because I don't watch TV regularly, so for me, this is a big treat. Generally, I prefer being active, creative, and focusing on other types of ways to pass time. However, when I have been on-the-go a little too much and I need a break, I'll sit and watch one of my favorite shows or a popular series I've been hearing about.

I've never watched an entire season in one day, but I have taken a few days to get caught up, and I must say, I love it. The best part about watching shows after the season is over is there is no wait to see what the next episode will reveal. No wait means less suspense. I like to get a bowl of popcorn, a few snacks, and have a much deserved, relaxing time.

31. **Do a craft.** There are many types of crafts to choose. If you will need a gift in the near future, you can make a handmade gift. If you're interested in creating new home décor, you can search for inspiration and then try to create your own version. If you have children, you can find a craft to do as a family activity.

I have updated the fabric on my dining room chairs, made wall art for every room in my house, painted a coat rack, and made home décor. Crafts can be very inexpensive or free, or they can be quite pricey if you let them. If you don't feel crafty, searching online for easy options that interest you may be a great place to start.

If you need a few ideas, I've compiled a list of crafts for your consideration.

- Paper Crafts – origami, greeting cards, or paper flowers
- Painting – canvas, wall murals, rocks, or t-shirts
- Drawing – doodling on paper
- Jewelry Making – bracelets, earrings, or necklaces
- Clay – small figures, keychains, shapes, beads, or pendants
- Embroidery/Sewing – ornaments, décor, clothing, or iron-on patches
- Home Décor – art or personalized items
- Nature Crafts – pressed flowers, rock art, leaf printing
- Candle Making

32. **Do a DIY project.** Crafts and DIY projects are very similar. However, every

craft is not considered a DIY project and vice versa. When I think of DIY projects, I think of building, modifying, or creating. Examples include furniture, home renovations, maybe a closet to increase storage space, or redecorating a space in your home.

I've created a list of DIY projects you may want to consider.

- Custom Wall Art
- Furniture – coffee table, chairs, or shelves
- Garden – vertical garden, raised garden, traditional garden
- Woodworking – décor, small furniture, or bird feeder

33. **Organize an area of your home.** You know the kitchen junk drawer, the one that has all sorts of random items that have nothing to do with the kitchen? Or perhaps there's a closet you have been avoiding, maybe a nightstand or a desk?

How about the kitchen table or the island if you have one? Maybe it's the pantry, or that pesky Tupperware cabinet, or the unkept shoe area.

Regardless of the space, organizing takes time and consideration. Most items in the kitchen junk drawer are there because they don't have a specific place where they belong. Finding a place for each item is key. Organizing can give you a rewarding feeling. When you are finished and can look at your work and know you made a difference, it's a beautiful feeling.

34. **Take a mental health day.** On this day, just breathe. That is the only requirement. That means no emails, no phone calls, no kids (if that's possible), no working, and do absolutely nothing you do not want to do. This does not mean don't enjoy spending time with your children if that is what you want to do, nor does it mean don't touch your phone if that will feel like torture. It just means no heavy lifting, mentally,

emotionally, and if you can help it, physically. Take a break from your norm, your work, and your chores. Do the things that make you the happiest or do nothing at all.

If cooking feels like a task on this day, choose not to cook, even if that means preparing your meals for this day in advance so all you are doing is reheating. If you generally check stressful emails and deal with all of life's problems first thing in the morning before you get out of bed, on this day, don't check your email at all. Guess what, those emails will be there whenever you get to them, so why not let them wait a bit. Odds are, none of them are urgent, even if the sender believes they are. For your mental health, it can wait.

35. **Use an oil diffuser.** Essential oils and aromatherapy have been in existence for centuries. While using oil diffusers in the home is relatively new, the benefits of essential oils have been debated for quite

some time. The benefits of these oils range from helping to ease the effects of mental health issues, such as anxiety and depression, to relieving or eliminating physical symptoms, such as insomnia, nausea, headaches, and much more. Essential oils are known to have healing abilities. I have found using an oil diffuser filled with water and a few drops of essential oil to be very relaxing. Similar to listening to soothing music, oil diffusers remind me of past visits to spas, and they set the tone of tranquility.

36.   **Burn a candle.** I love candles! Candles make me feel calm. You may think of a romantic evening when you think of burning candles, but even during the day candles can be soothing and mood transforming. Scented candles are the icing on the cake because they have the ability to take us down memory lane back to a familiar place or allow us to mentally travel to a place we'd like to be, like a spa or a vacation home. Apparently, it's the candle's low flame that allows the mind to

drift into a meditative state. Candles are one of the most affordable ways to reduce stress and raise your self-awareness.

37. **Watch one of your favorite movies.** Whether it's a classic movie from your childhood or a new release that you loved, allow yourself to stop for an hour or two and relax. You can make it a big deal and make popcorn, eat candy, and snuggle up with your favorite blanket or you can keep it simple.

38. **Pick up a new hobby.** In my neighborhood, the community center releases seasonal pamphlets containing a full list of activities for people of all ages. There are always classes and events at the community center, the local library, neighborhood parks, and local schools. There is something for everyone. If you have a little free time, searching for things to do in your neighborhood may be a good start. If it's close to home, your odds of continuing to do your newfound hobby are greatly increased.

Choosing a new hobby can be both overwhelming and exciting. Some hobbies align with our interests. Some hobbies are chosen based on the amount of free time we have. Budget, the level of physical activity required, and accessibility are also factors to consider when selecting a new hobby.

I've created a list of hobbies to help get your creative juices flowing.

- Reading
- Writing
- Painting
- Drawing
- Photography
- Gardening
- Cooking
- Baking
- Hiking
- Running
- Cycling
- Yoga
- Meditation
- Playing a Musical Instrument
- Singing

- Dancing
- Knitting
- Pottery
- Birdwatching
- Fishing
- Traveling
- Starting a Collection – stamps, rocks, wine corks, etc.
- Board Games
- Video Games
- Rock Climbing
- Scuba Diving
- Astronomy
- Model Building
- Volunteering
- Learn a New Language
- Blogging
- Vlogging
- Wine Tasting
- Playing a Sport – tennis, pickle ball, golf, basketball, etc.

39. **Go for a drive.** Going for a drive can be a good stress reliever for some. I have friends who go for a two-hour drive just to get out of the house. It's the change of

scenery that helps them. I also have friends who take a drive whenever their infant is fussy. A car ride is a great way to put a baby to sleep. If driving gives you anxiety or makes you feel road rage, then this may not be the ideal way for you to practice self-care.

40. **Stretch.** Stretching is good for the body and the mind. There are so many benefits to stretching that I've created a list.

Benefits of stretching:
- Helps reduce and manage stress
- Improves posture
- Eases muscle aches, pain, and soreness
- Improves range of motion
- Enhances coordination and balance
- Maintains flexibility
- Increases relaxation
- Mind-body awareness and connection
- Increases energy levels

41. **Plan a vacation.** Even if you don't go any time soon, planning a future vacation can be a ton of fun. If you do go, then that is even better. Planning builds anticipation and excitement. It gives the planner a path forward. This is helpful because we often spend the majority of our time looking backward, reflecting on the past, or forward, worrying about tomorrow and the days ahead. This exercise can be a stress reducer as it allows one to step away from the daily stressors and focus on a time they would love to have.

When children are young, we encourage them to use their imaginations. Yet, as adults we struggle with doing the same. We overcomplicate matters by overthinking, overanalyzing, and stressing. However, envisioning a relaxing or adventure-filled vacation offers the planner a priceless mental break.

Whether it is time to connect with family or friends or a solo adventure, taking time to reflect and create memories is valuable.

With work-life balance being a huge issue for many people, allocating time to ourselves is not only ideal but it should be mandatory. Vacations are for recharging. As humans, we burn ourselves out, especially those of us who are caretakers, either professionally or at home. Even if it isn't physical rest you need, we all deserve the mental rest.

For some people, the thought of planning stresses them out. If you are this person, I suggest two options; one, depending on how stressful planning is to you, consider choosing a different self-care activity. Self-care activities should be enjoyable to you, not stressful. Or two, use the following list of considerations to ensure a smooth and enjoyable planning experience.

Considerations when planning a vacation:

- Budget – Determine your budget for the entire vacation from the time you leave your door until the time you return. Be sure to include the following list in your budget.

- ✓ Transportation
- ✓ Parking
- ✓ Shuttles
- ✓ Car services
- ✓ Bus rides
- ✓ Flights
- ✓ Hotels or lodging accommodations – People are getting creative and finding new ways to stay near the destination of their choice.
- ✓ Activities – entry fees
- ✓ Meals
- ✓ Miscellaneous expenses

- Destination – You'll need to decide where you want to go. It is important to choose a vacation destination that aligns with your interests. If this part feels challenging, make a list of destinations. Then, either do what I would do, which is plan for each of them, or do the more sensible thing to do and narrow your options by creating a list of pros and cons for each. For example, if one destination is closer in distance and easier to reach, then that one may rise to the top of the list. However, if the closer one is also the most expensive, then maybe a destination a little farther but less expensive may take the lead. Either way, keep in mind that this just a plan, so keep all options open and don't limit yourself.

I had the extraordinary opportunity to visit Nairobi, Kenya, and it was an amazing, life-altering experience. I recommend anyone who wants to travel to a different country to do so. There is nothing like having the opportunity to immerse yourself in another culture with an open mind and eagerness to learn about the people, the food, the language, and the ways of life. I returned from Africa a different person, refreshed, renewed, and full of gratitude.

If Africa or another continent is not the goal for your vacation, that is perfectly fine. Wherever you decide to go will directly affect the timing of your vacation. A two-day driving trip is much easier to accomplish than a three-and-a-half-week vacation overseas, which brings us to the next consideration on the list.

* Time/Travel Dates – Part of the reason I suggested not to limit yourself is because you can control when this vacation takes place. If your vacation destination is overseas, then allow more time for planning and saving the money you'll need for your trip, but don't think this goal is unreachable. When it comes to travel dates, it is important to consider everyone's schedule. This part can be tricky. In my experience, the more time allotted for planning, the smoother the experience. Other time considerations include weather, seasons, special events at the destination, and your available vacation days.

- Packing Essentials – The way you pack can make or break the trip. It's all about being prepared for the unexpected. Smart packing is vital. However, if you are flying to your destination, be mindful of the airline guidelines as there are often hefty charges when the guidelines such as luggage weight are not followed. This may go without saying, but I'll say it anyway. Pack appropriately for the weather and activities in which you plan to participate. Forgetting swimwear when going to the beach or pool can be a costly mistake. The same is true for snow gear and keeping warm in the colder seasons.

Here's a brief list of packing essentials:

- ✓ Clothing
- ✓ Toiletries
- ✓ Travel documents
- ✓ Specialized gear based on activities
- ✓ Itinerary
- ✓ Emergency contact card

- ✓ Survival foods – peanuts, jerky, tuna, and other snacks
- ✓ Medication
- ✓ First Aid Kit
- ✓ Umbrella
- ✓ Extra shoes
- ✓ Anything else you may need

Popular Destinations Around the World

While this list may vary based on a number of factors, here is a list of popular locations.

- Paris, France
- New York, United States
- London, United Kingdom
- Rome, Italy
- Tokyo, Japan
- Barcelona, Spain
- Sydney, Australia
- Dubai, United Arab Emirates
- Bangkok, Thailand
- Cape Town, South Africa
- Rio de Janeiro, Brazil
- Venice, Italy
- Cairo, Egypt

- Bali, Indonesia
- Athens, Greece
- New Delhi, India

If traveling the world sounds amazing but feels too farfetched, don't be discouraged. There are plenty of ways to plan a trip or vacation locally. The sky is the limit, so have fun with this activity.

42. **Get dressed up for no reason**. The saying goes, "When you look good, you feel good." I have found this to be true. If you sit around looking pitiful, you will likely sit around and feel pitiful as well. If you take the time and effort to get up, groom yourself, and get dressed up, there is a possibility that you will feel amazing that day. If you doubt it, try it.

43. **Listen to a podcast.** Podcasts have been around for some time now, but for some reason, it took me a while to begin listening to them. Now that I do, I love how easily accessible they are and how

easy it is to search and find topics of interest. Podcasts open a whole new world of information, options, and entertainment, and it's all on-demand.

44. **Make your favorite dessert.** Baking can be fun. It's not always about the outcome. Sometimes it's the process that holds all the magic. Even if you don't want or need an entire cake or twenty-four cupcakes in your house, baking for someone else and delivering it to them can be rewarding for you and for the other person. It also counts as an act of kindness, so it's a two-in-one. If your favorite dessert is a no-bake dessert, then that makes it easier and still equally delicious.

45. **Declutter.** Having a cluttered space can add to your stress, anxiety, or feelings of overwhelm. Although decluttering may not be fun, the result usually feels great. Sure, you will need to figure out what to do with that thing you have no idea what to do with, but once you figure it out, you'll enjoy the clutter-free space. Oh, and by

the way, it's probably safe to say that thing, the one that doesn't have a place to go, may need another home.

Once the visual chaos disappears, you may find that the mental chaos disappears as well. Clean spaces offer a sense of calm, which allows mental clarity. It may literally feel as if you can breathe better once the clutter is gone. Have you ever walked into a room and felt calm vibes? Imagine that room being in your own home. Imagine feeling an instant burst of positivity whenever you walk into that room.

If the thought of decluttering overwhelms you, you should know it is normal for people to feel overwhelmed, stressed, or lost when it comes to clutter. If you need motivation, remember this: A cluttered space equals a cluttered mind, and a clear space equals a clear mind.

Here's a list of practical steps to make the decluttering process feel manageable.

- Start small—An entire room may be too much in the beginning. Choose a drawer, a single shelf, a table, or a closet. One tiny task at a time will help you accomplish your goals slowly but surely.
- Set clear goals—Define specific goals for your decluttering session. Goals can include a certain number of items or a certain amount of time. Clear goals equal to clear outcomes.
- Create categories—Sorting items into categories makes decision-making a little easier. You can have three piles: Keep, Consider, and Let Go. Items you undoubtedly want to keep can go in the Keep pile, items that may require a bit of thought can go into the Consider pile, and the Let Go pile can consist of donation items as well as those needing to be tossed in the trash.

- Set a timer—If you truly do not want to declutter but know it's needed, set a 15-minute timer. Fifteen minutes is better than zero.
- Ask for help – Sometimes, challenging tasks are easier when you have company. We can all use a little emotional support. If there is a significant amount of trash removal or decluttering needed, you may want to consider a professional service. There are trash removal companies that come out to do the dirty work for you for a small fee. If either of these options feels like too much to bear and makes you emotional, you may want to consider seeking therapy or counseling. A therapist will help you explore the underlying reasons for the clutter and develop strategies for letting go.
- Take breaks—If you need a break, take it. This process should not completely stress you out. If you need to walk away and get a snack or go for a walk and then come back, do it.

- Imagine the end result—Take a moment to picture what you want the space to look like when you are finished. This can motivate you to continue.
- Practice Positive Self-Talk and Self-Compassion – Be as kind to yourself during this time as you are to others. Celebrate the small wins. If you create a Let Go pile, be proud of that. Consider it progress. If you clean out a closet, do a happy dance simply because you are amazing. Remember, decluttering is a process. It took time to get the space the way it currently is, and it will take time to fix it. It's not a race, so be patient with yourself.

46. **Watch the sunrise or sunset.** I recently took a girl's trip to Florida. We woke up at 4:00 a.m. to drive an hour to the beach to watch the sunrise. It was a beautiful experience. I've also had the amazing opportunity to watch both the sunrise and sunset on airplanes this year as I traveled to Africa. I must say I've been really

blessed. Some may call it luck, but I know it to be a little more than that.

47. **Unplug.** I know how hard this can be for some people. I will not pretend as if it's an easy task for everyone. If you don't feel like you'll be able to go an entire day without electronics, what I recommend is starting slowly. Unplug for an hour. If that is easy, try three hours. Build your way up to a day. You will be surprised by the number of tasks that can be achieved when you don't have your phone glued to your hand, or the computer, video game, television, or whatever electronic device it is that has your attention.

Unplugging is simply refraining from using any electronic device for a specific period of time. This allows you to think more clearly, stress less, be creative, improve your relationships, explore new ideas, and more. Since we are often influenced by the world around us, unplugging can reduce anxiety and feelings of inadequacy, too.

48. **Get an hour of extra sleep.** We all need different amounts of sleep to feel rejuvenated. Whatever that amount of time is for you, give yourself an extra hour and see how it goes. This may mean going to bed an hour earlier, if possible. If this isn't possible, try the other end and set your alarm for an hour later. I recommend trying this on the weekend and not trying this on a workday, making you an hour late for work. That is not the goal here.

49. **Learn how to do something new.** This could be anything. It could be something you have always wanted to do but never seemed to make time for, or it could be something you just learned last week. Either way, it's never too late, and you're never too old to try new things.

50.	**Take an online course.** Courses are a great way to learn new skills. If you can think of a topic, more than likely there is a course on the subject. With so many platforms competing, online courses have become more affordable than ever before. Taking a course is rewarding and offers many benefits. A lot of courses are self-paced, which allows you to take the course at any time of day or night. Some offer a certificate of completion rewarded at the end to show off your hard work.

51.	**Treat yourself.** Think big or think small. Treating yourself to a cup of coffee is still treating yourself. It doesn't need to be a massive shopping spree. Some people neglect themselves because they don't think small enough. If budget is your concern, do something small. Go out just for dessert, pick up a manicure kit the next time you're out, or buy yourself a new (fill in the blank). These are all options of ways to treat yourself. Doing something small for yourself is better than doing nothing at all.

52. **Get a massage.** For some people, a massage is the ultimate level of relaxation. Many spas have specials when you purchase more than one service. Involve a friend and double the savings. Call around to see which place has the best deal for the lowest price. If price is not a concern, opt for the place with the best quality.

Benefits of getting a massage include:

- Stress relief
- Muscle relaxation
- Improved circulation
- Pain management
- Improved mood
- Better sleep
- Injury recovery

If you have underlying health conditions, it is recommended that you see a healthcare professional before getting a massage.

53. **Write a list of 5 reasons you are grateful.** There are numerous ways to execute this idea. You can get a piece of paper and a pen, a notebook, a journal, or even use the notes app on your phone. Try it once or make it a part of your daily routine. I recommend trying it for seven days. If that works well, try it for thirty days. Then, find a way to fit gratitude into your schedule regularly. Writing what you are grateful for trains your mind to be more optimistic and to search for the good which can be challenging for some people in the beginning. The more you practice gratitude, the easier it will become. You'll soon find it difficult to limit your list to only five reasons. When this happens, increase the number to 10.

Listing why you are grateful is similar to giving yourself a dose of sunshine each day. What you attract is what you get. Reflecting on the good will increase the good in your life. There will always be bad in the world, so deciding to find the good and focusing on that is a skill that takes practice. If you are looking to become a happier and healthier version of yourself, this is a wonderful place to start.

54. **Break from your norm in some way.** If you drive the same route to and from work every day, try a new route. If you go to the same grocery store every week, try a new grocery store. Find something small in your schedule and change it. Why? Breaking from the norm allows you to shake your schedule up a bit and to try new things. You may find that a new route to work lessens the overall time it takes to get there and back. A new grocery store may have new foods or lower prices. You never really know what you're missing until you try something new.

55. **Learn to sew, quilt, or crochet.** Sewing is a life skill. Too often these days, when something gets a hole in it, we just throw it away. That seems to be the norm. However, learning to sew can save money and can lead to a career as a seamstress, fashion designer, or stylist.

56. **Write a poem.** Have you ever tried to write a poem? Many people try to rhyme when they try to write a poem, but poems don't need to rhyme at all. There are many different styles of poetry. If you enjoy your poem, you may want to share it with someone.

57. **Write a random thank you letter.** A thank you letter is the perfect way to show your appreciation to someone. Saying thank you for being a good friend or thank you for always lending a listening ear are wonderful ways to brighten someone's day.

58. **Try learning a new language.** It's enjoyable to learn a new language, but it takes time, so this option requires a time commitment. However, once you begin to learn a new language, you open yourself up to new opportunities and experiences. There are thousands of languages in the world, and various factors dictate which language is most popular, including geographical location.

There are many ways to learn a new language. The method you choose should be based on your learning preferences. Here is a list of learning methods to consider.

- Apps and online platforms—Apps typically provide interactive lessons and exercises that can be accessed on demand at any time.
- Online courses and tutors – Courses and tutors online offer a one-on-one approach, or even if it isn't one-on-one, it is the human experience without being in person.
- Immersive language learning – Fully immersing yourself in a language is another way to learn the language. This can be any one of the following:
  - TV shows or movies
  - Music
  - Traveling abroad and speaking the language with the locals
- Traditional language classes – Some community centers or local colleges offer language classes. This

is perfect for the person who needs to be in person to learn.
- Books – Textbooks or other language-learning books exist. Visit your local library or bookstore to see what options are available.

Here is a list of 10 languages spoken around the world. They are not listed in any particular order; rather, they are listed to provide an idea of what language you may want to consider learning.

- English
- Mandarin Chinese
- Spanish
- Hindi
- Arabic
- Russian
- German
- French
- Swahili
- Romanian

59. **Skip checking emails for a day.**
Whatever is in your inbox will remain in

your inbox. Skipping a day will not hurt.
Most emails are not time-sensitive, and
even if there is one that happens to be
slightly urgent, the odds of the person
being able to continue working without
your immediate response are still very
likely.

60. **Read a magazine.** Sit back, relax, and
read about current celebrity gossip, the
latest trends, or any magazine you find
interesting. While magazines used to be
printed in paper format only, they have
evolved and are also online and can be
accessed through websites and mobile
apps.

61. **Visit a library or bookstore.** This can
be a family activity or a solo adventure.
You can go with an idea of a book in mind
or go with an open mind. I prefer the
latter. I have found myself in the
bookstore for over an hour browsing
through the books. Most libraries and

bookstores have seating areas, allowing customers to sit and read for a while. It can be very relaxing, and the change of scenery works wonders.

62. **Do a puzzle.** Jigsaw puzzles are perfect for any age. That's why they come in a variety of sizes and skill levels and range from a small number of pieces to a huge number of pieces. Puzzles should be challenging but not frustrating. Doing a puzzle as a family is a great way to spend time bonding away from electronics.

63. **Listen to an audiobook.** Sometimes we don't have time to sit and read a physical paperback or hardcover copy of a book. This is when audiobooks can really come alive. Audiobooks are typically the exact same wording as the paperback and hardcover and are often read by the author of the book. This is a wonderful way to read the book on the go while multitasking or sitting back and relaxing.

I listen to audiobooks as I drive, shop, and even when I cook. Audiobooks have allowed me to increase the number of books I read annually by a ton.

64.   **Practice positive self-talk.** This is one of my favorite forms of self-care. It doesn't require you to leave the house, write anything, or spend any money. It's simply looking in the mirror and speaking kind words to yourself, or you can skip the mirror and still recite kind words to yourself. While this exercise can feel a little silly, it is exactly what some of us need. We need to be comfortable speaking to ourselves in the way we speak to others and the way we expect others to speak to us.

65.   **Do something that makes you happy.** When asked what makes you happy, many adults have a difficult time answering the question. First, you may need to brainstorm and create a list of things that

make you happy. If this feels like a
challenge, this is normal. Keep going.
After you create your list, pick one thing
within your reach and do that one thing.
Remember to think small. It doesn't
always need to be a big idea.

66. **Have a Positivity Day!** A Positivity Day
is a wonderful opportunity to intentionally
infuse optimism and good energy into your
day. On this day, avoid using, speaking,
and even hearing negative words.
Depending on your lifestyle, where you
grew up, who is currently in your circle,
and many other factors, this may or may
not be challenging. A positivity day can be
specific, such as having a "no complaining"
day or a day of not using a certain word.
Whatever you decide to do on this day,
make sure that you are intentional and
take the necessary steps to make this day
successful.

Here is a list of what you can add to your
Positivity Day. Choose what works for you
and leave the rest.

- Start your morning by writing three to five reasons why you are grateful.
- Practice affirmations – focus on your strengths.
- Eat a healthy breakfast.
- Take a mindfulness break throughout the day – focus on your breathing, reset your mind, and do something calming (light a candle, use an oil diffuser, take a walk).
- Do a small act of kindness – compliment someone, help someone, or find a way to spread positivity.
- Visualize a positive outcome in your life – what does it look, sound, or feel like?
- During lunch, reflect on your day so far and think about one positive aspect of your day so far.
- Take a walk.
- Read a book.
- Listen to music that makes you feel happy.
- Surround yourself with positivity.
- Create a peaceful evening for yourself.

There are numerous benefits to being positive. Here is a short list, just to name a few.

- Improved mental health
- Reduced stress
- Lower rates of stress and anxiety
- Enhanced physical health
- Stronger relationships
- Better coping strategies
- Increased productivity
- Increased satisfaction

67. **Write five amazing things about yourself.** It can be easy to compliment other people. How easy is it for you to find five things you love about yourself and to write them down? Our inner critics tend to make us focus on the flaws or shortcomings making it hard to acknowledge and appreciate our strengths. Some of us fear receiving judgment from other people, so we remain modest even when we make giant-sized accomplishments. If complimenting yourself takes you out of your comfort zone, then maybe you should start doing it more often.

68. **Practice meditation.** Meditation is another topic that can be a separate book by itself. There are a plethora of ways to practice meditation, and the benefits range from emotional to mental to physical well-being.

Meditation promotes emotional health, helps with focus, sharpens memory, and increases self-awareness. Its stress-reducing abilities are mind-blowing. Meditation is also known to do all of the following:

- Reduces blood pressure
- Assist with pain management
- Aides in the mind-body connection
- Increases compassion and empathy
- Boosts the immune system
- Increase resilience
- Offers a sense of inner peace

If you have never meditated, it may be challenging at first. Meditation requires us to stay in the present, allowing ourselves to let go of the past, at least for a short time, and also to not think about the future. To make it easier, we focus on breathing, a word or phrase, the guide if there is one, or something around us, such as our senses. If your mind is often busy, slowing it down may take time and patience.

Some forms of meditation include:
- Mindfulness
- Loving-Kindness
- Transcendental
- Body Scan
- Guided
- Breath Awareness
- Zen
- Chakra
- Walking
- Mantra
- Gratitude

These are just a few examples and are meant to highlight the diversity of meditation practices. Meditation looks different for everyone, so if you try one method and it doesn't resonate with you, consider trying another until you find one that aligns with your goals. Keep in mind, there is no age limit and even children can meditate.

69. **Write five positive affirmations.**
Affirmations work simply because they challenge you to think positively, which counteracts negative and self-sabotaging thoughts. Repeating positive affirmations to yourself trains your brain to think positively and ignore doubt. Writing positive affirmations reprograms the subconscious mind. As we do this, we begin to believe in our own abilities, and our confidence begins to rise. This does not happen overnight. It's a process, but it can work if you're willing to do the work.

Here is a list of positive affirmations. Feel free to create your own. This list is just the beginning.

- I am loved.
- I am joy.
- I am worthy of love.
- I am worthy of acceptance.
- I am imperfectly perfect.
- I embrace my flaws.
- I am unique.
- I am enough.
- I am wonderfully made.

- I will achieve my goals.
- I am confident.
- I am capable.
- I am the designer of my life.
- My body is special, and I will take care of it.
- I am grateful.
- I attract abundance.
- I am open to receiving all good things.
- I am a light.
- I am peace.
- I am at peace.
- I will free myself from worries.
- I will attract good people, places, and things.
- I will uplift others.
- I deserve good things.
- The sky is the limit. I will keep reaching.
- Every day is a gift.

70. **Make a vision board.** Vision boards prompt you to look into the future, make plans, and dream. Creating a vision board can be a single-person project or a party

with a group of friends and family members. I have tried both options and loved them both. However, they yielded different results. As a solo project, I was able to focus on the board a lot more than I did when I hosted a Vision Board Party. Hosting involves a lot more planning, talking, and having a great time, so if you are thinking of trying this activity, think about the level of engagement you want to have while focusing on your future vision and let that be the deciding factor. And if you're anything like me, you can always opt for both.

I recommend searching online for inspiration, especially if you find this to be a challenging task or if your creative juices are not flowing. Some topics to consider adding to your vision board are health goals, career goals, learning goals, family goals, and vacation goals. Other ideas include a list of priorities, places to visit, bucket lists, and projects to do. Your vision board is just that, it's yours, so there is no right or wrong way to do it and no way to mess it up.

Did you know creating a vision board can offer the following personal and psychological benefits?

- Clarity – get clear on your goals, mindset, and visions, both short-term and long-term.
- Motivation – you are far more likely to achieve your goals if you can see them.
- Inspiration – having a visual allows you to stay inspired.
- Positive Mindset – Many people dwell on their past and get stuck in a place that no longer exists. By focusing on your goals and the positive outcomes associated with them, you are more likely to face challenges with optimism.
- Value Alignment – Your actions and values should be in sync. Feel free to add images of the values that guide your life so every time you look at your board, you get a gentle reminder.
- Personal Reflection – As you begin to think about your future, inevitably, you will think about

where you are now, what led you there, and how you can get from your current life to the one you envision. This process is self-reflection. As you become more self-aware, remember to be kind to yourself. Don't punish yourself with negative thoughts of how you wasted time or how you should have done this or that in the past. Focus on now and the future. You've got this!

- Positive Energy – By focusing on your goals, you attract good things and positive energy into your life. You invite new opportunities that align with your aspirations. Focus on good, and good will come.

Consider your vision board a tool for goal setting, self-reflection, maintaining or creating a positive mindset, and living a more intentional and fulfilled life. It's a roadmap to your dreams, so be intentional as you begin this process. Most of all, have a little fun with it.

71. **Make a photo album.** Either online or a physical book. Have you ever gotten together with family members and looked at old photos together? If so, you know the value of creating a photo album or at least the joy and nostalgia it could bring. Recently, I was in a popular store looking for a photo album and could not find one. This led me to believe that the digital world has caused a decline in physical albums. I checked several other businesses and found the same. While I was able to find one, the selection was nowhere near what it used to be when I was a child. If you're considering this activity, it may take some time to gather all the items you'll need to get started. If you're asking yourself what items you would need instead of pictures and the album, then you may not be aware of the varying levels of creativity in which this type of project can result. Other items include:

- Stickers
- Paper clips (for sorting and grouping images together)
- Decorative paper

- Embellishments – beads, pearls, gems
- Memory jar or box (for a less traditional style of collecting photos)

Viewing old photos will likely bring up a plethora of feelings. It's not a bad idea to add a box of tissues to the list. It can be emotional to look at pictures of places you've been or people you once knew who are no longer here. It can also be joyful, exciting, and fulfilling. Whatever this experience brings up for you, know that your feelings are valid and congratulate yourself for taking time to focus on yourself in the most unselfish way.

72. Make **a collage.** While a collage was previously mentioned, it doesn't necessarily need to be pictures. Creating a collage is a fun way to gather pictures, words, or ideas and group them into one fun project. This is another opportunity to allow your creativity to shine!

73. **Write a book.** There are so many people who have amazing stories to tell. Have you ever thought about writing a book of your own? Personally, I would love to hear your story. Yes, you! There are millions of other people waiting to hear it as well. If that isn't enough to get you to pick up the pen and paper, then how about this. Writing a book allows you to travel to a world in which you are the creator. This world can be as perfect as you wish, as realistic as you need, or as creative as your imagination extends. Getting lost in a world created by you can be therapeutic. Getting your thoughts out of your head and onto paper can relieve stress, and there really is no comparison to the feeling of completing a writing project and being able to write "The End."

74. **Start a collection.** Watching a collection build is always a satisfying experience. Imagine the joy you'll get when you somehow snag a rare piece of the collection. Now, think of when the collection is totally complete. Amazing,

right? Do you remember going on treasure hunts when you were a child? And do you remember how fun they were? Starting a collection can be compared to that, only you're older now. The fun, however, doesn't go away.

Here is a list of collections to consider:

- Coins
- Stamps
- Furniture
- Jewelry
- Art
- Books
- Paintings
- Sculptures
- Vinyl Records
- Toys
- Action figures
- Memorabilia
- Trading cards
- Minerals and gemstones
- Cars – model or drivable
- Instruments
- Dolls
- Watches

- Photographs
- Autographs

75. **Write a note to your future self.**
Imagine the future. How different do you hope the future will look from the present? Where will you be? Who will be there with you? Writing a note to your future self is both reflective and forward-thinking. Doing this exercise allows you to focus on your growth, goals, and choose who you want to be in the future.

76. **Give to a charity or support a cause.**
Donating to charity can positively impact the community, locally and globally. In some circumstance, it can save lives. Find a cause that is important to you. Maybe you don't have time to volunteer your physical time to help, but supporting financially or with goods (food, clothing, or other goods) can be just as helpful to the mission.

77.   **Surprise someone with a small gift**. I always use the example of leaving an unexpected tip for the server at a restaurant. While leaving a tip is customary practice here in the United States, depending on several factors, one being location, hospitality staff are often surprised when they receive more than twenty percent of the total bill. I have been a server and bartender before, and I know the feeling of needing the money I made from tips to make a living and feed my children. You can choose anyone to give your small gift. It can be a family member, a friend, a neighbor, or even a stranger.

78.   **Choose a day to be gentle to yourself.** On this day, only speak kind words. You've probably been your harshest critic for years. This day is the day to forget about your flaws, downfalls, and anything negative. It's your day to be kind to yourself. Tell yourself how amazing you are, how wonderful you have been, and

remind yourself of all the good things about yourself.

79. **Write for 5 minutes without stopping.** This is a writing exercise many writers do when they are experiencing writer's block. Writing for five minutes can also be therapeutic. It's a good way to do a brain dump and get everything out of your head and onto paper. Depending on what you are doing, five minutes can either seem like an eternity or it can feel as if it was only five seconds. So, what do you write when you don't know what to write? Good question. I'm glad you asked.

I usually instruct people to set a timer for five minutes and to keep the pen on the paper, and moving, the entire time. If you are using a phone or computer to write, then I recommend typing without stopping the entire time. If you have no idea what to write, that is what you should write. You will only write the words "I have no idea what to write" a few times before something else pops into your mind. Use this as an exercise to clear your head.

If you still have no idea what you would write, here are a few ideas.

- A To-do list
- A plan for the week (or the month if you're feeling ambitious)
- A letter to someone
- A letter to yourself
- A recap of the day

Keep in mind you only have five minutes. What you may find is you will go from not knowing what to write to not having enough time to finish what you started writing. That is a good problem to have. You can always start again later.

80. **Go for a bike ride.** Cycling strengthens your leg muscles as it targets your quads, glutes, hamstrings, and calves. It helps prevent and manage medical conditions and can aid in weight management, too.

Bike riding has a ton of benefits and is not only good for physical health, but mental health as well.

In addition to those wonderful reasons to hop on a bike, here are a few more:

- Reduce symptoms related to anxiety, depression, and stress
- Releases endorphins
- Strengthens concentration
- Develops awareness

It's a win-win. If you don't have a bike, a lot of communities have places that offer bike rentals. Your local gym will have stationary bikes. And with so many benefits, it may be worth the investment to consider treating yourself to a new or used bike.

81. **Go hiking.** Similar to cycling, hiking has both physical and mental benefits. You may wonder where to go hiking or who would go with you and if it's safe to go

alone. Those are all great questions. I've heard of many people hiking alone. Before heading out on your own, research the best places to go, the safety in the area, survival techniques, what foods or drinks to bring, and anything else you can think of that may help.

Here is a list of some of the benefits of hiking:

- Improves core strength
- Improves balance
- Regulates blood pressure and blood sugar levels
- Lowers risk of heart disease and a host of other medical conditions
- Improves cardiovascular health
- Reduces stress
- Enhances mood
- Strengthens and tones the body
- Supports weight management
- Enhances mobility and flexibility
- Offers an opportunity to connect with nature
- Social engagement, if going with other people

- Boosts energy levels
- Enhanced sleep quality
- Encourages mindfulness
- Strengthens the immune system
- Increases opportunities for adventure
- Impacts overall mental health
- Improves attention, creativity, and problem-solving
- Reduces mental fatigue
- Contributes to increased stress resilience
- Boosts self-esteem
- Reduces feelings of isolation
- Engages the mind and body
- Contributes to building emotional resilience

82. **Go camping.** There are varying opinions when it comes to camping outdoors. People who are adventure seekers and enjoy the thrill of the unpredictable weather and terrain consider camping a relaxing escape. Minimalists love the simplicity camping offers. Social campers love spending time with family or friends.

Then there are the people who do not find camping enjoyable at all nor do they understand how anyone else can. These individuals may seek a more comfortable, safer, and predictable getaway.

Regardless of which side of the camper you fall, a few things are undeniable. Camping allows you to slow down, breathe, detox from technology, and regroup. The entire experience is a chance to reset and give yourself the self-care you deserve.

83. **Go to a sporting event.** It is always fun to get in on the live action once in a while. The energy at sporting events is unmatched and cannot be felt as strongly when watching on T.V. Whether it's a basketball game, football game, baseball game, hockey game, or any other sporting event, so much time and planning go into hosting the event to make it the best possible experience for the participants. If you've never been to one, consider adding a sporting event to your bucket list. You

don't need to be a huge fan of the sport to enjoy yourself. You can always do a smaller local team instead of a well-known national team where there will be tens of thousands of people there, which can come with challenges. If you have been to sporting events and you love the idea, maybe try to go to one you wouldn't normally go to, such as seeing your football team in an opposing team's state.

84. **Go to a fancy hotel for a night. Order room service. Relax.** Chances are you have more responsibilities than you'd like to have, and chances are you handle every one of those responsibilities without realizing the true impact of all you do for everyone around you. Going to a hotel affords you the opportunity to relax in a way you probably don't do at home where a lot of those responsibilities reside. Ordering room service enhances the relaxation experience. All you need to do is decide which menu item(s) you want, find the remote, and temporarily forget about all of life's responsibilities.

85. **Buy flowers or a gift for yourself.** This one is short and sweet. It's simple. You deserve it!

86. **Go underwear shopping.** Shopping for underwear is more than just buying new clothing. Some people don't need a reminder and make it a regular practice to refresh their underwear collection. Then, there are those of us who may go in the undies drawer and find ten-year-old undies. It doesn't matter which group you fall into. What does matter is that we take the time to care for ourselves the same way we care for others. Keeping fresh underwear is also practicing good hygiene. If you need help remembering to buy new underwear, try a seasonal schedule buying a few pairs each season or maybe you'll want to buy more in one purchase to avoid needing to shop so frequently. Some moms buy the kids new underwear for back-to-school and then for Christmas. That may be another time to remember yourself, too.

87. **Watch a comedy.** Laughter is good for the mind, body, and soul. When you laugh, your body releases endorphins and trigger feelings of relaxation and well-being. Have you ever laughed because you heard someone else laugh? It's like the joy of laughter is contagious and spreads from person to person instantaneously.

88. **Splurge (within reason).** *Splurge* and *within reason* contradict each other a bit. However, if splurging reduces the chances of you achieving your financial goals, then don't do it. If you have extra money and will not be financially impacted in a negative way, then treat yourself. When was the last time you splurged? What did you buy? How did you feel before the purchase? And how did you feel after? Be mindful of your personal circumstances. There are 105 other ideas, so if splurging is not the one for you at this time, try another one that better suits your needs and current lifestyle.

89. **Go to a wine tasting.** Ever been to a wine tasting? Even though it's called tasting, there is a lot of tasting going on, so you may want to have a designated driver or plan to stay for a while.

90. **Hire a housecleaning service.** Even if it's a one-time deep cleaning instead of a regular service, do it! You deserve rest. If you are considering regular service, think of your pain points and delegate those spaces for someone else to do. It's more than just a time-saver; it's game changing. You'll get a clean house, more time to do other tasks or to relax, and a peace of mind.

91. **Create a playlist.** Music has a way of healing the soul. Even babies love music, and they often dance to the rhythm of the beat, naturally. The right kind of music can relieve stress and change your mood in a positive way. Having a playlist full of soothing songs can keep you uplifted and motivated. Be mindful of the music you listen to as certain types of music is

known to have a negative affect and cause stress and anxiety. The healing capabilities of music are so strong that some therapists use music therapy when working with their clients.

92. **Sit in silence.** Sitting in silence is very easy for some people and extremely challenging for others. Silence for an overthinker may feel like torture because their brain thinks it's playtime. They start thinking instantly, good thoughts, bad thoughts, silly thoughts, ridiculous thoughts, valid thoughts, and yes, unnecessary thoughts. The key to making this successful is to control those thoughts by intentionally focusing on something very specific. It could be your breaths, counting them as you inhale or exhale. It could be your body, starting from the top of your head and working your way to the bottom paying close attention to each body part as you silently name each one. It could be a goal you're currently working toward, planning each baby step you could take to get closer to the finish line. All

three of these techniques work extremely well. Your mind may still drift into other places. However, you can catch yourself drifting and refocus your attention to whichever option you choose to do.

When you allow yourself to sit in silence, you often gain clarity. You aren't just sitting quietly. There is so much more. You are allowing your body and mind to reset.

Here is a list of benefits related to sitting in silence:

- Reduces stress
- Improves focus and concentration
- Enhances self-awareness
- Promotes self-reflection and introspection
- Encourages mindfulness and being present
- Improves emotional regularity
- Promotes relaxation
- Improves sleep
- Improves decision-making skills

- Increases creativity

If these benefits sound amazing but you feel you may still struggle with sitting in silence, here are some helpful ways to overcome the most common challenges:

- Start small – Two minutes of silence is better than none. You can gradually work your way to sitting for longer periods of time.
- Set realistic expectations – Know that your mind may not clear itself of thoughts immediately. It is normal to continue to think about all sorts of things when you try to sit in silence. However, this gets better with time. Don't beat yourself up for thinking, and whatever you do, don't tell yourself not to think about whatever you've been thinking about. That is the quickest way for it to never go away. Instead, refocus your attention elsewhere, intentionally. Trust the process. It takes time.
- Focus on your breathing – Count your inhales and exhales. If you lose count,

it's okay. Remembering the number of breaths you took was never the goal. Rather, the goal is to have a point of focus.

- Acknowledge your unwanted thoughts – That's right. If unwanted thoughts arise, acknowledge them. Thoughts are a natural part of the mind's activity, and they don't just disappear easily, not until they are trained to do so. Say hi, and then redirect your attention to whatever point of focus you chose before you sat in silence.
- Create a comfortable environment – Trying to sit in silence in a chaotic, busy, or noisy environment can lessen your chances of success. The space needs to be conducive to relaxation. Keep in mind that this does not mean is the space large or completely clean. It can be a small nook, a closet, or a space not used very often, somewhere with minimal foot traffic and little to no distractions. Use cushions or blankets, if necessary.
- Be consistent – The best way to reap the benefits of sitting is silence is to do it consistently even if you feel it's not

successful at first. Consistency builds a routine, and a routine builds comfortability and confidence.

- Join a community – The truth is you don't need to do this alone. There are guided meditations and groups you can join. Sometimes, sharing the experience with people who are on the same level as you or people who empathizes with where you are can be helpful. They may offer techniques, such as mantras or soft sounds to assist with the process.

93. **Ask for help.** If you are used to being independent, not because you want to, but more because you've needed to, it may not be easy to request help. It may not feel comfortable. In fact, it may feel extremely uncomfortable and vulnerable. Maybe you're the type of person who has it all together. You may have heard the saying, "Check on your strong friends." And you may be that strong friend who helps others rather than needing help yourself. If this describes you, I completely understand how challenging it may be to

ask for help. However, it is important to note that life has a funny way of happening. Sometimes, we are up and guess what, there will be times when we are down. As the comedian Martin Lawrence stated in a popular comedy concert, none of us are immune to the trials and tribulations of life. To think we will never be on the receiving end of needing help is not realistic. If we don't learn that lesson early enough, we may wake up one day and find ourselves in a deep, dark, unfamiliar place.

I have good news! You are not stranded on a desert island and there are people who would love to help you, but you need to allow them the opportunity. By doing so, you may resolve your issues and while doing so, you may strengthen your relationship with your family member, friend, or whomever the person is who was able to offer support. Asking for help prevents isolation reducing the risk of social withdrawal. Even if the person cannot help themselves, they may be able to collaborate with you leading to more effective problem-solving. Perhaps they'll offer new ideas and creative solutions. While some may feel asking for help is a sign of weakness, it is an empowering choice. It demonstrates self-awareness and the courage to prioritize your well-being.

94. **Watch the company you keep.** Have you surrounded yourself with positive, productive, successful people who inspire you to be the best version of yourself? The company you keep is more important than some people realize. Each person brings a certain level and type of energy. Energy is contagious. Good energy seeks good energy, but guess what? Bad energy also seeks good energy only for different reasons, typically to destroy it. The saying misery loves company is true. People with toxic energy can drain positive energy turning into negative energy in the most subtle, undetectable way. You may have family or friends who you love with all your heart but may need to distance yourself from them to protect your own

energy. Take time to analyze your circle of friends. Take note of who receives most of your time and decide if that person is someone you admire or if they bring out the worst in you. This process can be challenging but it's vital to maintaining your mental well-being.

95. **Search for inspiration.** Look outside of your comfort zone. Doing so will give you a fresh perspective. Moving outside your comfort zone can be as simple as trying a new item on a restaurant's menu to something as adventurous as skydiving. As it relates to inspiration, trying something new can lead to new adventures, new relationships, and new ideas.

96. **Pay it forward.** Paying it forward is an expression for when the beneficiary of a good deed repays the kindness to someone else instead of the person who did the first good deed. For example, if someone buys you a cup of coffee and says, "Pay it

forward," they are requesting you to do something kind for someone else. It's a chain of good deeds that makes everyone involved feel a little happier.

Have you heard of random people who secretly pay the bills of other random people? I remember there was a person going to popular stores that offered layaway programs. For those who don't know, a layaway program is when a person chooses the items they would like to buy, but instead of leaving the store with the items, they pay a small percentage of the total which commits the store to holding the items for a specific period of time until the person can come back to the store to pay in full.

Well, there was a person going to these stores and paying the balances for people they didn't know. This act of kindness gained media coverage, and it was really awesome, and inspiring, to see kindness taking place in this way. You don't need to mimic this person, especially if it is not within your means to do so, but a small act of kindness can go a long way.

97. **Smile at someone.** Have you ever received a smile from a complete stranger? Depending on where you're from, a random smile can either be normal, common courtesy or it can be extremely strange. In inner cities where people are often way too busy than necessary and always rushing like there's no tomorrow, seeing random smiles from strangers is less common than more rural areas that are naturally slower paced. This does not mean that city people are mean and country people are kind. However, in a busier environment, people are often focused on several tasks at once, and may not take the time to be in the present moment long enough to consider sending a kind gesture such as a friendly smile. This is not to make excuses for anyone's rudeness; rather, it's to point out different states of mind and awareness people tend to be in on a day-to-day basis. There are many other factors as well. The next time

you're out, give someone a big bright smile. You may find that smiles are contagious.

98. **Compliment someone.** Making someone feel good about themselves will make you feel good too. This option is quick, easy, and free.

99. **Take a day trip.** Whether you're a busy person or someone whose life is calm, your days are likely routine. You probably wake around the same time every day and follow the same schedule. A day trip is a great way to change your pace, routine, and focus. They can be adventure-filled or relaxing. You should decide based on your needs. Do you need more action and spontaneity, or do you need a break from the action and just want to rejuvenate your mind, body, and spirit? Take a moment and think to yourself where you would go if you could take a day trip today. Who would you allow to go with

you? Would you drive, take a train or bus, or maybe a bike or a plane?

Your creative juices are probably already flowing, but just in case they are not, here is a list of the benefits of taking a day trip:

- Relaxation
- Stress relief
- Physical activity, if you choose adventure
- Quality time, if you take loved ones
- Creates memories
- Increases creativity and inspiration
- Improves mental health
- Encourages a healthy disconnect
- Contributes to personal growth

100. **Relax.** The world is so fast paced we often forget to relax. We are constantly trying to meet the demands of work, parenthood, and other responsibilities that we put relaxation on the back burner with no intentional plans of returning to check on it. So, what happens? We keep going until

we have nothing left to give. We experience burnout, which forces us to relax, only by then we are in such a deep state of need that relaxation alone isn't enough. Let's break that cycle. If you don't already, start scheduling relaxation time on your calendar to relax. During that time, do whatever relaxes you. Let's stop reserving relaxation and looking at it as a luxury and let's start using it as a tool to balance and live a more fulfilling life.

101. **Give to someone less fortunate.** There are billions and billions of people on earth and many of them need help in one way or another. Giving to others provides a sense of purpose and fulfillment when done with good intentions. Helping others can also provide a broader perspective on life leading to feelings of gratitude and humility. You don't need to be rich to help people who are less fortunate. When I was at my worst financial state, I helped people because I knew God would provide for me. I made kits filled with socks, shampoo and conditioner, other toiletries,

and snacks for people who needed them. I also volunteered my time at the local community cupboard to assist with my time instead of money. The experience I gained and the fulfillment I felt for being a useful, helpful member of the community is priceless.

102. **Be gentle with your expectations of yourself and others.** Having very high expectations of people, including yourself, can cause frustration. We often place unrealistic expectations on ourselves or other people and then wonder why we feel let down. In these instances, we were not set up to succeed. It is totally fine to have standards but make sure they are realistic from the start.

103. **Rearrange your space.** Rearranging your living space can positively impact your life, mood, and ability to think clearly. For example, decluttering contributes to mental clarity and reduced stress. Rearranging furniture can improve the energy flow and create a more inviting,

relaxation station type of feel. Changing the way your space looks can lift your spirits, remove feelings of stagnation or monotony, and create the environment you aspire to have. Additional benefits include enhanced functionality, aesthetics, and adding your personal touch.

104. **Make a list of all the things you love.** Trust me, this one is a no-brainer. This list can include anything, your children, favorite drink, best coffee shop, your favorite movies, literally anything. Then, put the list somewhere close, near your workplace, on your closet door, bathroom mirror, etc. Each time you pass the list, take note of one item on the list and smile as you lean into a memory of that person, place, or thing. This cute activity boosts your mood and fills you with gratitude and joy.

105. **Make a list of goals.** Do you have your goals outlined on paper or in a digital

device, or are they in your head floating around? It is so important to take those goals from your head and put them in writing. Be very specific and intentional when creating your goals. Make sure they align with who you are as a person and more importantly with whom you plan to be in the future. Do your best not to be vague about your goals. After all, your life depends on it. Once you have your goals written or typed, you can categorize them into short-term and long-term.

Here are examples of specific, intentional short-term goals:

- Exercise for 30 minutes three to four times a week
- Saving a specific amount of money each week for a specific purchase
- Eat homemade meals three to four times a week for one month
- Spend 20 minutes a day learning a new skill or working on a hobby
- Start and finish a book within a month

- Drink the recommended amount of water for a month
- Connect with a friend once a week for a month
- Create a budget and stick to it for three months
- Declutter one room or space each week
- Volunteer in the community once a month
- Complete a course within the next two weeks
- Use one hour less screen time for two weeks
- Take a ten-minute break from work daily to walk or stretch
- Start a gratitude journal and spend five minutes using it daily
- Establish a daily routine that includes self-care
- Prioritize sleep by establishing a bedtime routine and going to bed on time
- Introduce a new food to your diet weekly

- Reduce portion sizes of carbohydrates and increase vegetables

Short-term goals should be realistic and achievable. Use one of these or create your own.

Here are examples of specific, intentional long-term goals:

- Pay all debt and achieve financial independence within five years
- Build an emergency fund worth 6 months of expenses in the next two years
- Lose forty pounds in one year
- Make a lifestyle change to eat more healthily removing all processed foods
- Purchase a home within the next five to ten years
- Travel to a new country within the next three years
- Advance in your career and reach management level or upper management level within the next five years

- Earn an advanced degree or certification in your field within the next two years
- Diversify your investment portfolio to achieve long-term financial goals
- Create a life that offers more balance between work and life, somehow prioritizing well-being and professional success
- Master a musical instrument within five years

Long-term goals are more extensive and typically span months, years, or decades. Some long-term goals are easily achievable but require time, and other long-term goals are more challenging and ambitious, requiring significantly more effort. These are sometimes referred to as reach goals and may include running a marathon, launching a successful new business, or writing a novel.

106. **Go on a date alone.** Simply put, you are worth it!

This chapter was all about determining what self-care could look like for you. You may have noticed that some of the ideas were easy in terms of complexity and quick to complete, while other ideas were grandiose and would take a lot more time and effort. Choosing the right form of self-care for the time you have in your schedule is key. If you only have ten minutes to squeeze in self-care for the day, opt for easier, less time-consuming options, such as listening to your favorite song, writing five things you are grateful for, or smiling at someone. Overcommitting can leave you feeling burned out, which could lead to the false assumption that there isn't time for self-care.

We have learned that there are many ways to practice self-care that only take five minutes, yet there is still that chance that some of us will skip a day, week, month, or even a year of self-care before realizing it. Some of us will blame it on lack of time. And let's face it, our schedules are tight. Many of us are busy from the time we wake up until the time we finally get back in bed to rest again. While timing is critical when deciding how to practice self-care, there is something even more important than timing. I'd like to share a secret with you. I will tell you, and then hopefully, you will share it with someone else. Are you ready? Here goes. Our lack of self-care has almost nothing to do with a lack of time. The real reason we don't practice self-care regularly is that we don't prioritize our lives and schedules effectively. Sometimes the truth hurts, so let's examine this theory.

Mothers, empaths, and helping professionals often take care of everyone around them, leaving themselves for last. I would like to pause and take time to recognize that there are wonderful fathers and many other individuals who also fit into the category of people who prioritize everyone else first, leaving their own care last. However, the three examples I cover in detail in the upcoming chapters include mothers, empaths, and helping professionals. It's important to me to include everyone because the topic of self-care is universal. No one is excluded or exempt from the benefits of caring for themself, and the same is true when it comes to the disadvantages of neglecting oneself.

- While self-care looks different for everyone, there is no doubt there is something for everyone on the list in Chapter 8. Whether it's shopping, creating, outdoor activities, indoor activities, or spending time searching within, there are over 100 ways to practice self-care. Which will you choose?

- Budget does not determine if a person can practice self-care. It only helps to narrow the options. If budget has ever stopped you from practicing self-care, I challenge you to count the number of self-care activities that do not require money. Sometimes, we just need to reframe our way of thinking and stop selling ourselves short. Make today the day you focus more on what you can do and less on what you cannot.

- Self-care activities can be done in a group, or they can be done alone. If you don't have anyone to do activities with, then either do some things alone. While you're out, you may meet new, interesting, and fun people. Whatever you decide, keep in mind that your self-care journey is yours alone. Make the absolute best out of it!

- Fitting self-care into a packed schedule can feel impossible at times. Unsuccessful attempts to do so can force us to believe time is the issue. We learned the real reason we struggle in this area, and in the upcoming chapters, we will begin to unpack this theory.

Notes

Notes

Notes

Notes

Chapter 9

Mothers

Being a single mother, I personally know the struggle of trying to balance life and all it encompasses. I have been caught in the whirlwind of being a working professional, taking care of the kids, cooking dinner while helping with homework, cleaning up random messes, attempting to have a social life, driving the kids to and from activities, and trying to further my education all at the same time. I would be lying if I said I've always made time for self-care. At some points in life, in my mind, there simply was no time for anything else. I was barely handling my responsibilities efficiently enough to feel good about them. Adding something else, anything else, seemed nearly impossible.

Mothers naturally put their children's needs before their own. Obviously, this isn't true for all mothers, but I am speaking for the large majority who take the role of motherhood very seriously; the ones who make it their duty to love, nurture, and protect their children from the first time they lay eyes on their babies. For many women, it happens even sooner than that. It could be the very first time she hears the baby's heartbeat, or when she notices the baby bump for the first time, or when she feels the baby's first kicks, or for me, it was when one of my pregnancy screenings came back unfavorably.

When I was 16 weeks pregnant with my first child, my quad screen, which is a prenatal test that analyzes four substances in a mother's blood, came back abnormal. My doctor called me herself to inform me that there was a chance that my daughter could be born with spinal bifida, that she could possibly have a hole in her spine, and that she could possibly be paralyzed from wherever the hole was in her spine all the way down the rest of her body. While she described the chances of this happening as one in some huge number like 1,380,000, to me, it seemed as high as one in three. It was in that moment that my motherhood instincts kicked in and I fell in love with my unborn baby. I also panicked upon receiving the news while at work. I hyperventilated and broke down crying. I remember the doctor asking me to repeat back what I heard her say. I am not sure she expected the reaction I gave. I surely was not expecting the reaction I gave.

The mere thought of anything being wrong with my child threw me over the edge. That was the day I fell in love with Jadyn Milaan. And so that I don't leave you wondering what happened, Jadyn was born five months later, happy and completely healthy. She ended up practicing cheerleading starting at a young age and continued all throughout high school as a flyer on the team. In high school, she founded the dance team and cheered simultaneously. The team is still going strong today, even though Jadyn graduated and went off to college.

Now on the other end of that spectrum is the mother who needed some time to learn to love her child. For this mother, maybe she dealt with postpartum depression unexpectedly. Maybe the child was the result of unforeseen or uncontrollable circumstances. Maybe this mother never saw herself having children, or perhaps she was never shown what love and nurturing look and feel like. Maybe she's fearful. I have spent many years working with mothers who have suffered from postpartum depression. One thing I have learned is that most mothers love their children with everything in them. However, when a person is suffering from mental health challenges, and on some days she feels as if she can barely take care of herself, motherhood can seem impossible.

Discussing motherhood is so important to me because, from my experience, no one is harder on themselves than a mother. We are constantly wondering if we're doing enough, if we've done too much, if we are doing the right thing, if we have done the wrong thing, if we are giving too much, if we are giving enough, and the list goes on. We give and give selflessly, often without being thanked or appreciated. Yet, because we feel it's our job, we continue to give more than what we even have in us to give at times, almost always putting ourselves last.

Message to Mothers

Hey, moms! From one mama bear to another, I want you to know I see you. Your hard work and dedication to your children is nothing short of amazing. Yes, it gets hard, and no, people don't always understand. Just keep pushing to be the best person and mother you can be. That doesn't mean to pour from an empty cup. It means the opposite. It means to take time for yourself each day. Fill your cup by taking care of your mental health. Do something for yourself, even if it's for five minutes. If you need help figuring out what that looks like, go back and revisit Chapter 8. There are tons of ideas that will help you fill your cup. Children deserve to have a wonderful mother, and you cannot be the best if you aren't taking care of yourself just as much and just as well as you're taking care of everyone else. Be good to yourself. Be patient with yourself. Be kind to yourself. You deserve it!

Notes

Notes

Chapter 10

Lisa

L isa is a mother of two children. She works a corporate job and makes a decent living. She's comfortable with home and work life and does her best to balance the two. Lisa used to love dancing. She used to take dance lessons, and music was once a huge part of her life. Lisa also enjoys gardening, social gatherings with friends, and traveling, none of which she currently makes time to do.

After having children, Lisa focused most of her attention on her children. They are only two years apart, so home life is busy, to say the least. Eating healthily is important to Lisa, so she cooks most of the family's meals. Eating out is also expensive, so Lisa takes that into consideration as well. The oldest child attends piano lessons, and the youngest child is on the swim team. Lisa played the trumpet when she was a child and wanted her children to learn to play an instrument, too. She was excited upon realizing the youngest seemed to be a fish in the water. However, being on a swim team takes a lot of time during the week leaving very little time for any other activities. Overall, Lisa and the children live a good life.

A couple of years pass, and Lisa realizes she no longer does all the things she used to do. Instead, she's knee-deep in being a mother, which she loves, but she also realizes that she's lost her sense of self. A friend mentioned the words self-care to Lisa, and she shrugged her shoulders and stated, "What's that!?" in a sarcastic voice. To Lisa, people who need self-care are people who are mentally ill or on the verge of breaking down. Lisa felt as if she was completely fine, had everything under control, and just needed to find her identity. She felt as if she had temporarily lost her identity and planned to go online and order a new one, or at least that's what she said jokingly to her friend. She truly didn't see a need for self-care. She barely knew what self-care was and thought of an expensive trip to the Caribbean when she heard the term self-care. Immediately dismissing the thought, Lisa thought to herself, "I don't have time for that. With this busy schedule, that will never happen."

While Lisa jokes a lot, inside, she really knows she needs to do something differently. She is starting to feel sad, confused, and like she doesn't know what she should be doing with her life. She searches online for "How to find yourself," but doesn't have time to read the blogs or watch the videos she finds, so she continues to live life the way she has, taking care of the children, working, and cooking.

One day, Lisa noticed she'd been short-tempered with her children. That morning, she yelled at the oldest child for spilling milk on the counter. Work was becoming stressful, and Lisa was losing interest. The same evening, she yelled at the youngest child for leaving shoes in the middle of the floor and "being messy." Lisa felt horrible for being mean to the kids but also felt like they were always making messes, and she was always cleaning up the messes. Lisa was tired. Exhausted. She needed a break. She knew she needed a break but didn't take the time to take one. Instead, she continued her regularly scheduled programmed life; cooking, cleaning, working, and momming.

As you can imagine, there came a day when Lisa looked in the mirror and no longer recognized the person looking back at her. The identity that was once temporarily lost was now completely, and what felt like permanently, lost. Lisa cried like a baby. She looked in that mirror, and she ugly cried real tears. It was at that moment on that day that Lisa knew she needed to change. She could no longer go on living life the way she had. She'd become bitter and sometimes a little snippy. It wasn't intentional, and Lisa didn't really notice how differently she'd been acting. Lisa called her best friend, the one who had previously mentioned self-care when Lisa had scoffed at the idea. She cried to her friend, explaining how hard life is and that she's tired of everything. The friend listened with open ears and could feel Lisa's pain. This time, instead of telling Lisa what she needed, she asked Lisa if it was okay to make suggestions or if she just wanted her to listen and not speak. And this time, Lisa was more receptive than she'd ever been. She was in an extremely vulnerable state, had hit rock bottom, emotionally, and was open to try anything to get out of the dark space she'd fallen into. Lisa was willing to listen.

Surprisingly, her friend gave the same advice she'd previously given. She told Lisa that it is not healthy to spend every second of the day taking care of everyone else besides herself. For the first time, Lisa agreed. Working hard at work had taken a toll on Lisa. She would leave work and immediately jump into mom mode. Lisa left no time in the schedule for Lisa. Lisa's amazing friend showed her this book, the one you are reading now, and said, "Start here." Lisa loved chapter 8 because it opened a new world for her, one that taught her the importance of remembering herself, loving herself, and taking care of herself. They talked about how time seems to disappear into thin air. They discussed prioritizing Lisa over anything and anyone else, even if it's for short periods of time. Before the end of the conversation, Lisa began to feel better. She felt a sense of hope, excitement, and appreciation.

1. Lisa's friend, who remains nameless, immediately recognized Lisa's need for self-care, but like many of us, Lisa didn't see a need for self-care. After all, she was busy, and life wasn't "that bad." However, we must realize that life doesn't need to be bad before we consider loving ourselves enough to pay attention to our own needs.

2. Like many people, Lisa had a misconception about self-care, who needs it, what it means, and how it could help her. Lisa thought two things: Self-care was not for her. It was for people who desperately needed it, and self-care meant taking lavish trips to foreign land, neither of which are true. Yet, many people believe these myths to be true, so they neglect themselves until a crisis is presented.

3. Like many people, Lisa began to feel the effects of neglecting her own self-care. It was gradual, but inevitable. Lisa had gotten to a point where she didn't recognize herself. Her mood was affected. Her relationships were affected. Work was affected. It was time for change.

4. Lisa waited until there was a crisis to consider change. This is exactly what many

of us do. This way of living forces us to be reactive rather than proactive. It's much easier to slowly infuse self-care in your life now than it is to do the deep work of recovering from years of neglect later.

Notes

Notes

Chapter 10

Empaths

E mpaths are people who can feel the feelings another person is experiencing. They are deeply tuned in to other people's emotions. While most humans can and will experience empathy at some point in life, empaths feel empathy on a deeper level and can be greatly affected by the people around them. There are many types of empaths, but we will discuss nine types.

- Emotional Empaths – Whether good or bad, an emotional empath feels the emotions of the people closest to them, but they can also feel those of strangers, too. Emotional empaths are naturally compassionate. They may seem as if they are always aware of other people's moods and can easily absorb the mood they sense someone else is experiencing. These empaths may cry often or cosign their friend's anger when someone has wronged them. They celebrate wins regardless of who's winning, and they feel sadness as they can easily relate to or understand sad situations. It is important for this type of empath to learn to regulate their emotions as they can easily feel stress or compassion fatigue for wanting to help others. Learning to set boundaries is a must for this type of empath.

- Intuitive Empaths – These empaths sense energy and emotions when people speak and through body language. They experience high levels of empathy. Intuitive empaths are typically wise, logical, rational, and caring individuals who are often guided by their hearts and brains.

- Physical Empaths – A physical empath can feel the pain another person is experiencing in their own body. If someone bumps their knee or stubs their toe, this person can feel the pain in that part of their body.

- Dark Empaths – This may be the worst kind of empath. Dark empaths feel a high level of empathy but use it to prey on others. They are manipulative and use the feelings of others to serve their own needs and will use what a person says to get what they want.

- Plant Empaths – These empaths feel connected to plants. They always know what their plants need to stay alive, and they feel a bond with their plants.

- Animal empaths – Similar to the plant empath, an animal empath feels a great connection with animals. They understand the patterns and cues of animals and can easily sense when animals are sick or if something is off.

- Earth Empaths – These individuals feel a deep connection with the earth and are sensitive to nature's changes. Earth empaths may become excited at the site of a waterfall or energized upon seeing the sun. They often enjoy the trees in a park, the waves in the ocean, and the birds in the air. They may also be saddened or feel sick at the smell of air pollution, thunderstorms, or gloomy days. Earth empaths may experience Seasonal Affective Disorder (SAD) and become depressed during the winter months when the daylight is shortened.

- Heyoka Empaths – While these empaths are rare, they are known to be the most powerful. They use humor and are socially defiant. Their empathy level is so high that they can mirror people perfectly. They don't mind showing their dark side and typically prefer to be alone.

- Super Empaths – These empaths are a narcissist's worst nightmare. They are fully aware of their identity and will set boundaries. They can exhibit traits of all the other empaths and don't typically give in to social pressures. Super empaths use their intuition and attempt to avoid burnout. They are good with animals and pets.

Most people have a challenging time navigating their own feelings and emotions. Can you imagine feeling what everyone else around you feels as well? Sounds exhausting, right? From experience, I can tell you it is extremely exhausting and if you are not careful, it can lead to a deep, dark place. This is why I chose to focus on mothers, empaths, and helping professionals. If you fall into any one of these categories, you need self-care like your life depends on it.

How to Tell if You're an Empath

- Do people tend to tell you their problems?

Empathic people tend to be skilled listeners, naturally. People are often comfortable in their presence. They are well-trusted, and people easily share their deepest secrets with them without much prompting. If this is you, be very careful. Empathic listeners are often manipulated and vulnerable to toxic behaviors. People will often tell you what they want you to hear, omitting the parts of stories that show their faults. It can be easy to fall into the trap of a disingenuous person if you are blinded by your own sincere desire to help.

- Do you have a heightened sense of intuition?

Have you ever just felt like something was off? You didn't have a concrete reason. There was nothing physical that showed you that what you were feeling was true, but somehow you just knew. It was as if you could feel it in the air. Well, that was your intuition. Empaths tend to have excellent intuition but may not always act upon their feelings. Being caring individuals, many empaths will ignore signs of doubt and will give the person the benefit of the doubt simply because they want to see the good and hope for the best in people.

- Are crowds overwhelming?

Most empathic people do not enjoy crowds. They prefer quiet, calm environments, surrounded by the people they care about. They are usually natural introverts.

- Are your senses heightened?

Do you find that certain places are too loud for you? Do you prefer to listen to calm music, or at least have your music at a low volume? And for television, do you prefer a lower volume, or to not watch it at all? How about your sense of smell? Are there fragrances that are just too strong? How about other odors? Are you affected by them more so than the people around you? All of these are examples of ways in which the world around you could be affecting you. Empaths often have increased sensitivity in these areas that are totally unrelated to emotions.

- Do you find yourself needing time to recharge?

While a load of negativity can drain even the most upbeat and optimistic person, the same can be true for an overload of positive emotions. Taking on everyone's emotions can be exhausting and draining. It is important to stop, take a rest, and recharge. Neglecting to do so can lead to burnout very quickly.

- You avoid conflict.

This one is interesting because it happens so naturally. There is a link between avoiding confrontation and being an empath. We all know there are people who like to argue and fight, but let's just assume most humans do not enjoy fighting and would rather get along. Empaths most likely dread confrontation and avoid it altogether, if possible. Additionally, empaths are very sensitive people. They may be easily offended. Criticism may be taken personally, and snarky remarks may be more offensive to them than to others. Coping with conflict may be challenging.

This is not an all-inclusive list, so if you feel you may be an empath, it's worth doing more research to protect yourself from compassion fatigue, burnout, stress, and more. Being a caring person who can feel the emotions of others is not bad. It would be a wonderful world if everyone could be a little more empathic and could spread a little more kindness. However, being an empath and not knowing it or being an empath and failing to include self-care in your regular routine is unhealthy.

- Due to an empath's deep ability to feel what other people can feel, it is crucial to protect themselves from becoming overwhelmed with feelings of exhaustion, compassion fatigue, and stress.

- We covered nine types of empaths and the areas in which their senses or feelings are heightened.

Notes

Notes

Chapter 12

Shawn

Meet Shawn! Shawn is a young man in his mid-thirties. He works for the government and makes a fairly good living. Shawn has children and loves being a father. He loves sports and plays in an adult league in his free time. When he isn't working, Shawn is an active member of the community and volunteers to help children from lower-income neighborhoods. He enjoys taking long rides, soaking in the sun, and sitting in silence, which allows him time to think. Shawn is an empath.

At work, Shawn is well-liked and has been the go-to person for a lot of his coworkers for years. They tend to feed off his positive energy and take turns confiding in him. The same is true for Shawn's relationships outside of work. His work in the community has made him a popular person around the neighborhood. Random people approach him and share stories that most people would only share with their closest friends. At the end of each day, Shawn often feels drained from fixing everyone's problems. He listens to music to wind down and reset. Then, he wakes up and offers the same help to anyone who needs it the next day. Shawn is different from Ciara and Lisa because he takes time for self-care. He goes to the gym regularly to exercise, and even though his friends go to him to help with their troubles, the relationships are mutual, and he goes to them for a listening ear just as much.

The problem with Shawn is even though he is aware of his need for self-care, he struggles with setting boundaries. If anyone needs him, he's there. Even when he is not available, he makes himself available. Putting on a cape and saving the entire world, or so it seems, can only go so far. Even though Shawn takes time to fill his cup, he often finds himself pouring more into others than he does himself simply because he lacks the ability to say no. Some of us can relate to Shawn. We give and give so much of ourselves that we end up feeling exhausted with giving. We know giving is good, so we feel conflicted when we feel like we don't want to give any more or we don't have anything else to give, mentally, emotionally, or physically. This is where setting boundaries comes into play.

The truth is that no one can be available to everyone all the time. Being ALWAYS ON is draining. The best thing Shawn or anyone in this position can do is to have some OFF days; unplug, say no, be unavailable, and just rest. These days should not be random. They should be scheduled weekly for as many days as needed. An example of what this looks like is saying, "I am not available on Saturdays or Sundays for the next few months." No other explanation is needed. This statement lets someone requesting time know that you are not available and it's not negotiable. Another example is saying, "I need to see when I will be able to do that. Let me get back to you." This is not saying no, but it is saying that you may have other obligations and you will consider their request when time allows. It's worth noting that if you use this example, you should really take the time to reach back out to the person with your availability and don't just blow them off. You want to set boundaries without losing friends.

By setting boundaries, you can balance life a little easier. You won't need to fill your cup as often because you aren't pouring out as quickly. Instead, you are allowing yourself time to relax, slow down, and breathe. It is important to know that setting boundaries and limiting your emotional and physical availability is not selfish. In the beginning, when you first pull back your availability, you may feel like you're being selfish. After all, you have been giving selflessly for years, so growing out of that may not be easy. Don't let that feeling discourage you. It gets easier with time. Take the time to get to know yourself better. Start doing things for yourself. As for Shawn, he realized that his work in the community, although admirable to many, was taking so much time that he barely spent time with his children who were growing up fast. He started taking time to hang out with his children all together and individually. He found that the time he spent with his children was valuable time and he was extremely pleased with himself and his decision over time. It was not easy for him to be unavailable at first. But when he sat and thought about it, he realized that saying yes to one thing meant saying no to another thing. He didn't want family time to be the thing he said no to, and that made the process much easier. Now, Shawn has Daddy-daughter dates with his daughter, he plays basketball with his son, and occasionally, when everyone is available at the same time, he gets them all together for family activities. As a result, Shawn's life feels whole, and he doesn't feel the exhausted feeling of taking on everyone's problems. He is able to pour into work, the community, and his family, and he loves it.

Let's Recap

1. Shawn's story is unique because he is an empath and realizes it, so he takes time to practice self-care, yet he has difficulty with setting boundaries.
2. Saying no makes Shawn feel selfish, which leaves him on a hamster wheel spinning for dear life. Since he practices self-care, he

should be good, right? Not quite. If you're pouring from your cup faster than you can fill it, you will still eventually end up pouring from an empty cup.

3. Setting boundaries is a crucial step in self-preservation and self-care. By making a schedule and blocking times when you are not available, you allow yourself to pour a little slower, thereby reducing the speed at which your cup becomes empty. The goal is to always have something in your cup. The cup is a metaphor and represents your mental, physical, and emotional capacity as well as your energy level. Keeping your cup full is comparable to keeping your battery charged. If your battery is low, you cannot function optimally. If your battery dies, you're no good to yourself or anyone else. So, let's keep those cups full and the batteries charged.

Notes

Notes

Chapter 13

Helping Professionals

A helping professional is a person who takes care of the needs and well-being of other people for a living. Many careers fit into this category, so here is a short list to name a few. This list does not fully cover everyone who fits into the category, so if you feel your career fits, then this message is for you, too.

Helping Professionals

- Doctors
- Nurses
- Medical Assistants
- Counselors
- Therapists
- Coaches
- Teachers
- Psychologists
- Psychiatrists
- Attorneys
- Childcare Workers
- Hospitality Staff
- Social Workers
- Case Managers
- And more

Helping professionals often put the needs of other people before their own needs. They wake up and check emails, prepare for meetings, or begin working even before getting out of bed. They have the overwhelming task of managing schedules at work and at home and struggle with feeling appreciated for their hard work in either location. These feelings of unappreciation stem less from reality and more from personal feelings of guilt, knowing they are pulled in multiple directions at once, leaving them unable to be fully present wherever they are. Constantly multitasking weighs heavily on the helping professional. Juggling work and home life often leads to neglecting their self-care needs, and trying to balance it all often makes them feel incompetent regardless of their accomplishments, skill level, or education level.

If you have been reading this and wondering if a person can be a mother and an empath, or if an empath can also be a helping professional, or if a person can be all three simultaneously, the answer is absolutely, positively, yes! For the mother or father who is also an empath and a helping professional, I salute you. Your job is not an easy one, and you deserve self-care in every form. You owe it to yourself to protect your peace at all costs. You are an angel on earth and will benefit greatly from the self-care activities listed in Chapter 8.

Notes

Notes

Chapter 14

Toya

Y ou have already met Toya. She is me, and I am her. I've already shared a bit about my personal life, but we can recap briefly and then go into a little more detail about my most current events. I thought it was appropriate to add my chapter here just after the previous chapters on mothers, empaths, and helping professionals because I happen to be all three. I am a mother of three. I've been an empath all my life, and for twenty years, I worked in a helping profession. My life experiences have equipped me to be able to write this book with such conviction and to share the message of the importance of self-care. In the introduction and Chapter 1, I explained how I went in for a regular doctor's visit, vented about my life, and left diagnosed with depression. If you skipped the intro, you may want to go back and read it. I also explained how I had no idea the lifestyle I was living was causing me to feel the overwhelmed feelings I felt or that I could take certain actions to change my life for the better. I didn't know about self-care at the time, not like I do now, and I would have told anyone who mentioned self-care that there was no time for that in my busy schedule.

Back then, my oldest child was five years old, and my youngest was one year old. Today, my oldest is 18, and the one-year-old is now 14. I also added one more to the bunch during the COVID-19 global pandemic, and she is now four years old. I'd like to sit here and say that after 13 years, I have mastered self-care, and I never need reminders to take better care of myself. I'd like to be able to say that being diagnosed with depression was the wake-up call I needed, and since that day, I have prioritized myself and my well-being. I would even like to be able to say I learned from my mistakes with my first two children, and since having the third one, I no longer make mistakes or forget to practice self-care. However, none of that would be totally true. In fact, when I first wrote this book years ago, I thought I was finished, and I put the book up for preorder. Then, I felt an extreme urge to pull the book from preorder and not publish the book at that time. I totally disagreed with the urge, but it wasn't just an urge. It was deeper than that. It wasn't fear or a lack of preparedness, and this may sound strange to anyone who is not spiritual, but personally, I knew it was God telling me not to publish the book. So, as much as I disagreed with the urge, and even though I did not understand why He would stop me from publishing the book, I knew I needed to be obedient, so I pulled the book off preorder, and I did not publish it at that time. It didn't make sense to me, but we will get back to that in the final chapter. Reluctantly, I sat the manuscript to the side and focused on other areas of life.

Shortly after that, COVID-19 shocked the world. No one expected a global pandemic to shut down the world or to change it in the ways it did. I was eight months pregnant when the media first started covering the pandemic. I was just about to stop working due to maternity leave, so I had already planned to be home for the next few months. What I didn't know or plan was for my children and everyone else in the world to be on maternity leave with me. But again, no one did. Like everyone else, I had to adjust... everything. In the beginning, many people didn't take the pandemic seriously. Some thought it was a conspiracy, a hoax, scare tactics, and so on. Being eight months pregnant, I took it very seriously, especially when the news channels began sharing that doctors were contracting COVID-19 in hospitals. I knew I needed to go in to deliver my baby within a month's time, and the world was falling apart. It was by far the scariest time of my life. It was also when my anxiety began. About a month later, my baby girl was born. It was the worst hospital experience and birthing experience I have ever had, yet after her birth, I had the deepest feelings of peace than I had ever had. At that time, the hospitals were changing their policies on how to handle the pandemic daily. Everyone was confused, scared, and no one felt safe. Delivering mothers were not allowed to have a support person with them until after they were admitted to the hospital. The catch was that I was not admitted until it was almost time to push the baby out, so I went through all of the pain associated with giving birth alone. I truly was not admitted until 20 minutes before my daughter made her appearance, and there were so many emergencies that morning that the doctors and the anesthesiologist were not available. I could hear nurses calling for doctors to respond to emergency births over the loudspeaker. Because of the policies, confusion, and emergencies, I was forced into a natural birth, which was not the plan. The entire experience was traumatic and was just the beginning of what was to come.

I stayed home with all three of my children for a year and a half. The older two went to school virtually like the rest of the world. When they had an opportunity to go back to school in March 2021, I chose to have them stay home out of fear that they would bring COVID home. We lived in an apartment at the time, so each child had an area for school that was fairly close to the others. My daughter was set up in the living room, and my son was set up just a few feet away in the dining room. My son plays the trombone and his music class was also virtual. I remember getting the baby down for a nap and then hearing the blaring sound of the trombone shortly after. It was quite a time. Within that year and a half, self-care took a backseat to everything and everyone. I shared a bedroom with the baby, so there was no alone time. She woke up a lot throughout the night and discovered very quickly that my bed was a better place to sleep than her crib. She wasn't much of a napper during the day, so there wasn't much downtime. The two older kids played outside a lot. Other than that, the only place we went frequently was the neighborhood grocery store. Just to get out, I went shopping for groceries multiple times each week. It was a scary, stressful, anxiety-provoking time.

Due to the intense level of stress I endured daily, my blood pressure rose. As a result, I needed to take medication to control it. Since different medications work differently for each individual, I became what felt like a guinea pig as I learned which medication would be the one for me. The first one worked great to control my blood pressure, but it also made my tongue swell. I was allergic to the medication, so my doctor switched me to another one. The second medication worked, but I was allergic to that one too. That one made me feel like I was going to faint. I took it for months feeling unsteady and afraid. Finally, I realized it was the medication that was making me feel that way. So, we tried a third medication, hoping the third time would be the charm, the one that would work. The third medication helped to lower my blood pressure, but it also increased my anxiety, gave me heart palpitations, and lowered my potassium. I ended up needing to see a cardiologist about the palpitations. He explained that the medication was the cause of the palpitations and that if I were to continue taking that medication, I would need to also take potassium supplements. My doctor switched my medication to a fourth medication. This medication was gentle. I didn't feel any side effects, and I was not allergic. However, it was not enough on its own to control my blood pressure. We needed to combine medications to give me the right combo that would lower my pressure. After some time, what felt like lots of time, we found the right combo and I began to feel much better. As you can imagine, during the time of finding which medications would work, I fell into a dark place. My anxiety was so high that I'd been back and forth to the Emergency Room and Urgent Care nearly a dozen times. I started having panic attacks and needed to be rushed to the Emergency Room twice. I called a friend the first time I had a panic attack, and she rushed me to the hospital. Another time, I needed an ambulance. A third time, I attempted to drive myself, which was a very, very bad idea. I drove about halfway to the hospital and had a very serious panic attack. My heart started racing as fast as it could. It was thumping. I needed to stop the car and call the police. After some time, they sent an ambulance, and the ambulance took me the rest of the way. It was a horrible, terrible time.

The panic attacks were the result of several thoughts. First, one of my sisters passed away from a stroke in her forties. Knowing that high blood pressure can lead to a stroke made me feel as if the same thing that happened to my sister could also happen to me. That thought caused a lot of fear. It felt like a never-ending cycle. I would worry, and worrying would instantly raise my blood pressure. Then, I would panic because my blood pressure was high. The panic only made my pressure higher. The highest I remember was 179 over 102, and I was in the back of an ambulance. What a horrific experience that was.

The other thoughts included feelings of helplessness and lack of control. I could literally think myself into a panic attack, and I had very little control over my thoughts at the time. The nurses in the Emergency Room gave me medication to calm me down. They sent me home with twenty pills to help with anxiety. The pills worked like a charm. My blood pressure was normal, and my anxiety was under control. When I went to visit my doctor to tell her the good news, she did not seem thrilled about the pills and did not want to prescribe more. I didn't understand why. Instead, she talked to me about lifestyle changes and other medications to consider. I left the doctor's office feeling informed but also confused. I didn't understand if the medication from the Emergency Room worked, why wouldn't I continue to take it?

Then, I randomly, very randomly, had a conversation with a girl I'd met a few years prior. She told me how she'd just gotten out of rehab because her anxiety was so severe that she kept going to the Emergency Room. Our stories aligned at that point, so I tuned in to the conversation intently. When she would go to the Emergency Room, the doctors would give her the same pills they gave me. She became addicted to the medication and kept going back to the Emergency Room specifically to get more pills, and they kept giving it to her. Her addiction caused her to need to be admitted to a rehab facility for weeks, nearly a month. It turned out that my doctor was protecting me from addiction, and I didn't even know. I ended up having a conversation with my doctor about it, and she explained that the medication is sneaky. She said it works without a doubt, but it is for emergency situations, not for daily use. We had a long, informative conversation, and this time, I left feeling grateful that she saved my life. I am so grateful that she did not prescribe more of those pills because my family has a history of drug abuse and addictions, and that very well could have been me needing rehab, even though my intentions were innocent. Whenever I went to the Emergency Room after that, I was very cautious about what medications they were giving me.

Throughout this time, I tried to lower my blood pressure in other ways aside from medication. I removed sodium from my diet as much as I could—sodium is in almost everything. I started eating as healthily as I could, but that had no effect on my blood pressure. Between the baby weight and what I call COVID weight, my weight played a huge role in my blood pressure being so high. I gained approximately forty-five pounds and weighed more than I ever had. Even though I had a gym at the apartment, finding the motivation to exercise was a struggle. I knew I needed to lose weight, but I didn't know how I would do it. The thought of it just added more stress.

I want to point out that not many people knew I was going through all of this. Naturally, I am a happy, optimistic, outgoing person. No one knew the struggle I had going on behind the scenes. This is just one example of why checking on your strong friends is important. I am the strong friend. I am the one people can come to when they need a listening ear, words of encouragement, advice, and so on, but I am also human, and I go through the struggles of life just like everyone else. When I take pictures, I typically smile. When I posted pictures during this time of my life, they would be of the happy moments I found throughout that day or simply a pose. The pictures did not truly reflect who I was at the time or what I was experiencing. They showed a happy, excited-about-life version of me. If you have a friend you haven't talked to in a while, take a moment to check on them. It could be a simple message saying, "Thinking of you," "How are you doing?" or "Just wanted to let you know you're in my thoughts. Have a great day!" Those random check-ins can mean the world to someone who needs their cup filled.

You may be wondering how I overcame all of that or if I am still going through it now. Well, I had several wake-up calls.

Wake-up Call #1

When I went to the cardiologist, I noticed all the patients were seniors, and then there was me. I'm sure there are other young patients who visit that office, but on that day, it was obvious I was the only patient in my thirties. Everyone else appeared to be between 65 and 95 years old. I knew I needed to change.

Wake-up Call #2

Another wake-up call was realizing that my sister's health and mine were not the same and that I was worried about something that I didn't need to be worried about. I'd let the thought of death consume me. At my lowest point, I wrote a letter to each of my children and sat it next to me before I went to bed. I feared when I went to sleep that night that I would not wake up the next day and I wanted to leave them each a message to remember me. I had no indications in my own life that I was at severe risk of having a stroke or dying, but I felt like it could happen today or tomorrow, and the fear was more than I could handle.

Wake-up Call #3

Remember when I mentioned going to the Emergency Room nearly a dozen times? Well, if that isn't a red enough flag, the staff started to recognize me from previous visits. That's never good at a hospital. One of the nurses carefully and kindly approached me and gave me a paper with resources to speak to a counselor or therapist. It was as if she wasn't sure what my reaction would be, but she wanted me to know there was help if I was willing to accept it. I responded, "Thank you! I wholeheartedly believe in therapy." I wanted to hug her for being so gentle in her approach. I really appreciated her, and while she probably thinks she was just doing her job, it meant a lot to me.

Wake-up Call #4

The first time I ended up in an ambulance was because my friend, who rushed me to the hospital during my panic attack, took me to a children's hospital because it was the closest hospital to us. It's slightly laughable now, but at the time, not so much. Apparently, if an adult goes to the children's hospital needing care, the protocol is to call an ambulance. If you have never been in an ambulance, let me tell you, it's a scary experience. I don't watch T.V. much, but I definitely started thinking the worst thoughts, such as how do I know they will actually take me to a hospital or what if they harm me in some way. I was an emotional and mental mess. However, Gibbons, the EMT, was the kindest, sweetest person ever. He talked to me, asking questions to gather as much information as he could without making it feel like an interrogation. He explained that I was fine and that I was going to be fine. Gibbons made the experience as easy and calming as it could be.

Let's fast-forward to the panic attack I had while attempting to drive myself to the Emergency Room. The panic attack occurred in the middle of a national park, making it a challenge for the ambulance to find me. When they found me, I had calmed down a lot. After getting into the ambulance, I realized that I recognized the face of the EMT. It was Gibbons. There I was once again going through the same horrible experience, and there was Gibbons once again talking me through it. As friendly as Gibbons was both times he rescued me, I did not want there to be a third time.

Wake-up Call #5

The last wake-up call was when I realized my diet had nothing to do with my high blood pressure. If I had eaten any healthier, my food would have tasted like cardboard. That's when I knew for sure that my issue was stress, and I needed to reduce my stress like my life depended on it because it did.

Notes

Notes

Chapter 15

Prioritizing Self-care: Non-negotiable

M oving to a new location was amazing! It was the change I needed to propel my family and me to a better future. I was able to take my mind off negative, stressful events and focus on home décor, furnishing the house, color palettes, and starting over. It was a complete reset. But as amazing as the new house was, I knew it wasn't the full solution to my problems. It was a large part, but there was more. I needed to get to the root of the problem. I needed to make prioritizing self-care a non-negotiable in my life.

I conducted extensive research on stress and anxiety. People often talk about them as if they are one and the same, and they aren't. Stress is a physical, emotional, or mental reaction to a change or challenging experience. It is a natural response, and most humans encounter some level of stress throughout their lives. Occasional stress is a normal coping mechanism. However, prolonged stress, also known as chronic stress, can contribute to or cause a host of health problems. Anxiety is a feeling of worry, fear, or uneasiness. While anxiety can occur as a reaction to stress, it can also occur without the presence of stress and without any obvious triggers. Many of the symptoms of both are identical. However, there are some symptoms that differ.

Symptoms of Stress include:
- Dizziness
- Muscle tension

- Digestive issues, including nausea and diarrhea
- Anger
- Irritability
- Trouble sleeping
- Headaches
- Increased Sweating
- Feelings of overwhelm
- Change in appetite
- Increased heart rate
- Restlessness
- And more!

Symptoms of Anxiety include:

- All of the symptoms above
- A feeling of impending doom
- Tingling
- Numbness
- Brain fog

I assumed my anxiety was the main problem because I assumed I had my stress under control. Being a single mom, I was used to being stressed, so I focused on the newer of the two issues: anxiety. By the way, notice how I said I assumed I had my stress under control because I was used to stress. So many people have that way of thinking, and it's truly sad. Enduring stress for a prolonged time doesn't make us experts at managing stress; rather, it can cause more serious issues later, as it did for me. If you or someone you know is stressed, please take it seriously. Share this book with them or share another resource because stress is dangerous.

During my research, I learned that anxiety presents itself differently in each person and that there are varying levels of severity. I also learned that there are many ways to treat anxiety, including medication, therapy, self-care, and nutrition. When I compared the treatments for anxiety and stress, they were similar. While medication is an option, it's a personal choice, and some people would rather not take that option. As for therapy, I believe everyone needs a therapist. Even the therapist needs a therapist. The problem with this option is that it can be expensive, and not everyone can afford a therapist. When it comes to nutrition, there are foods that are known to reduce symptoms of anxiety. However, this option may or may not be effective for some people, not to mention, changing the way we eat can be challenging for some people. So, I began to focus more on self-care.

I was shocked to learn that practicing self-care is a proactive way to prevent stress, anxiety, burnout, compassion fatigue, and all sorts of health issues. During my research, I kept looking for answers to my questions on how to cure myself or how to get rid of stress and anxiety. The one answer that kept coming up for me was self-care. I learned that there was no magical fix. There was nothing that could make it all go away overnight or within weeks. I learned the hard way that it takes time. I didn't acquire stress and anxiety overnight and I was not going to get rid of either of them overnight. It was going to be a journey. While that was a hard pill to swallow, it was the final wake-up call I needed to begin prioritizing self-care like never before.

Doing good for others is not the problem, per se. In fact, doing things for others can be a form of self-care in some instances. The problem comes when we spend so much time caring for others that we forget or simply fail to care for ourselves. Self-care is not something that should be added to the bottom of the list. It should not be something we do if there is time left in the schedule. And it most certainly should not be something that we push off, allowing ourselves to be neglected while we put on a cape and save the rest of the world.

If you are like me and need to take better care of yourself mentally, physically, or emotionally, follow along with me as I explain how to prioritize self-care. The solution is very simple, not always easy, but it is simple. Self-care must be a top priority. Don't wait until you're in desperate need because even though it won't be too late, being reactive, is not a good feeling when you could have been proactive.

So, here goes. Here is how to fit self-care into an already-packed schedule. Imagine you have a blank calendar. Before you begin to fill your calendar with everything you plan to do for everyone else – the doctor's appointments for the kids, the vet appointment for the dog, work deadlines, or whatever else you have included in your busy schedule that prevents you from being able to practice self-care—the calendar is a blank slate.

From the blank calendar, choose a day of the week. Declare that day as your self-care day. Now even though we are pretending to start with a blank calendar, if there is a day of the week that does not work with your schedule, I recommend avoiding that day. The purpose of this exercise is to set yourself up for success. Being realistic with yourself and with what you will be able to achieve is a huge part of this journey. On that day, select from the list of self-care ideas listed in Chapter 8 or think of one of your own. Consider how much time the self-care activity will take and block that amount of time on your calendar. Planning in advance can be extremely helpful. On your calendar, mark that day and time as SELF-CARE DAY - NON-NEGOTIABLE. Self-care must become first on your to-do list. That, my friend, is the secret. Once you successfully complete a week of self-care activities, decide how often you want to add self-care to your calendar: daily, bi-weekly, weekly, every other week, or monthly. Get good at it. Make it a game. Make it a habit.

Beware of Falling Off the Track

Once you establish a pattern for practicing self-care, beware of falling off track. As I have shared, I still need reminders from time to time. A few years ago, I went to my doctor for an annual checkup. Yup, this again. This time, she asked what I did for self-care. I drew a blank. My realizations always seem to come when I go to doctor's visits. It had been a decade since my first doctor's visit where this all began, and here I was, sitting in another doctor's office with another doctor, needing to be reminded again. I would like to say this was the last reminder I needed, but it wasn't. It took many reminders, many times of falling off the track, and many times of caring for everyone around me better than I was caring for myself. What I noticed was that every time I fell off the self-care track, the consequences worsened.

When I attempted to answer the question, I was really dumbfounded and needed to think for a minute. After a minute, I needed a few more minutes. Maybe it was the spur-of-the-moment unexpected question that had me stumped, or maybe it was the fact that it is easier to care for everyone around me than it is for me to remember to care for myself. Either way, I realized the need to do better. There was a sudden fire burning within me to take care of myself, to be intentional about self-care, and to practice what I preach.

I constantly speak to women about self-care. I tell them what they should be doing, could be doing, and even how to make things better. I go as far as to tell people to put self-care as number one on their to-do list, yet here I was stumbling to figure out what it was that I do for my own self. When I mentioned this to my doctor, we laughed. She completely understood and shared that not all doctors are good patients. That also reminds me of the hair stylist whose hair is never styled or the therapist who fails to seek therapy. Sometimes it's just easier to help others and forget about ourselves.

So, How Do We Stay on Course When it Comes to Self-care?

As the seasons change, so will some of the options for self-care. For example, if you enjoy taking walks in the spring and fall weather but don't like being out in the cold of the winter or the heat of the summer, you might need to find other ways to practice self-care in the winter and summer. Some people get into routines and then allow something out of their control, such as the weather, to alter the routine. The person who takes outdoor walks during the spring might fall off track on the first eighty-degree day. For this example, making a plan in advance for what to do on hot or cold days is a great way to stay on track. I have gone to the mall when it first opened and have seen seniors walking laps around the mall, so maybe taking the walk indoors is an option. Maybe instead of walking on those days, an online exercise session could be an option, or maybe swimming is a good option in the summer to keep cool or create a do-it-yourself workout in the winter. The point is to keep moving and adapt to any changes or obstacles that may come your way. If you are not prepared for possible obstacles, you could easily fall back into old habits of neglecting yourself. Preparation is key! Make appointments with yourself to review your self-care calendar often. If weekly appointments feel like too much and monthly appointments aren't necessary, try quarterly. Every twelve weeks is a great time to realistically ask yourself if what you have been doing is working for you, if what you said you were going to do is actually what you are doing, and what you can do to improve. If you realize you fell off track, no worries. You can simply hop back on at any time.

If you need to set reminders, use any reminder tool that will work for you. You can make a short list of self-care activities and put the list in a place where you will see it often. You can also use a reminder app or a tracker to track how much progress you have made. The tracked record should serve as a motivator to remind you how much you have gained from your new self-care practice or how much more effort you need to put into sticking to the process. It can also show you if the approach you took is not working as you thought it would, so you can do something different.

Scheduling Self-care Assessment Meetings

I recommend starting with monthly meetings. Find a time when you will have 20-30 minutes to yourself. Ask yourself, *"What would I like to do for self-care for the next month?"* Choose from the list of options provided in chapter 8 or think of some of your own ideas. Make sure the day you say you're going to practice this act of self-care is a day that you actually have time to do so. Be as realistic with your goals as possible, so that you have a better chance of achieving them. Decide the frequency of your self-care goals. Then, go as far as blocking that day and time on your calendar. Treat your Self-care Assessment Meetings and your self-care goals as importantly as you would if they were someone else's tasks. Come back in a month and do another assessment of your goals.

Understand that it may take time to adapt to the process. If you are not good at practicing self-care, like I wasn't, it's possible that you may struggle to stay on track in the beginning. This is totally normal. Remember, Rome wasn't built in a day. It takes time to get into a new habit, and in most cases, it takes even longer to let go of an old one. Don't let slip-ups make you feel like it's impossible. You've got this!

If something doesn't work, find out why it didn't work. Was your goal too big? Did you go from zero self-care to massively overloading your schedule? That is one sure way to get overwhelmed and to fall off track, so start small. If everything goes well in the first month, congratulate yourself. Be happy and celebrate yourself for taking care of yourself. I believe in celebrating small wins. If there were scheduling issues, that is okay. Just be more intentional next time. Be careful when selecting the day or time to avoid double booking or other scheduling issues. If there are any unforeseen issues, reschedule, refocus, and resume your self-care plan. It really is that simple. Try not to spend too much time harping on what you did not accomplish. Just try again.

Keep in mind, if you continue to prioritize self-care as last, it will always be either the last to get done or worse; it will never get done at all. No one else is going to put your self-care first, so this one is on you. Start small. Look at the list from Chapter 8 and see which option you can choose right now. Do that one activity and count it as you moving one step further in your self-care journey.

- Self-care can be a part of the treatment plan for people dealing with stress or anxiety. By practicing self-care before experiencing health issues, you are being proactive. If you experience health issues as a result of a lack of self-care, your self-care journey is more reactive than proactive, but learning to take better care of yourself is vital to your healing process.

- The secret to fitting self-care into a busy schedule is to make self-care a top priority. Before you start filling up your calendar with appointments, events, and work, choose one day to be your self-care day and stick to that decision. On that day, make self-care non-negotiable.

- Sometimes, we fall off track. That is totally normal. Don't beat yourself up about it. The moment you realize you fell off track is the moment you start a new beginning. "If at first you don't succeed, try, try again."

- Be flexible. Understand that things won't always work out as planned so prepare for any obstacle that might come up.

- Schedule Self-Care Assessment Meetings. These meetings will help you determine whether what you're doing is working or if you need to try something else.

Notes

Notes

Chapter 16

A Better Version of Me

And here we are! Remember in Chapter 14 when I mentioned how I attempted to publish this book a few years ago and something told me not to do it? I explained how I originally wrote this book, placed it on preorder, and then felt the urge to take it down and wait. I had no idea what I was waiting for, but I was told to wait, not by a person, but by a higher power, and so I did. At that point in my life, I had not experienced all I needed to fully be able to tell my story. While I didn't understand the "urge" to stop the book from being published at that time, now that I have lived and experienced so much more of life, I can truly say I get it now. It is time to spread the word about self-care and how important it is for all of us. I realize now that the original version of the story ended as if I had all the answers. I ended with, "And that is how you do it!" Not literally, but that was the tone of the message. The harsh reality was that I was not finished learning, experiencing, or even writing this book. As it turns out, becoming a better version of myself is a work in progress, and I don't have all the answers. In this chapter, I will share what has worked for me up to this point in hopes that it works for someone else, too. I no longer want to claim to have it all together, and if sharing my story of vulnerability helps someone else become a better version of themselves, then I am humble enough to share it.

What I did to become a better version of me

Overcoming anxiety

Overcoming anxiety was not easy, but it was a choice I made. I refused to continue to be a victim of my own self-destructive thoughts. While I considered medication, I wanted to try other methods first. I am not against medication, but I wanted that to be the last resort and only take that option if all else failed. Once I found out the pills the Emergency Room gave me were addictive, I was careful about taking them and used them only in emergency types of situations.

Knowing that some anxiety is normal, I allowed myself to feel those feelings and work through them. The feelings came and went, but the more I accepted them and faced them head-on, the less fearful the feelings became. I found helpful videos online to learn techniques to ease anxiety. I also started therapy, practiced box breathing, and jumped head-first into self-care. I want to point out that the process was not easy or quick. There were moments of feeling hopeless and down. During those moments, I would remind myself to be gentle with myself and to take it day by day. I used to tell people to take it one day at a time, and when that was too much to take it hour by hour. This time I gave myself that advice.

Overcoming stress

Overcoming stress is still a work in progress. My research on how to get rid of stress was extremely interesting. I kept looking for the easy way out. I wanted to find the answer that would make the stress disappear within a few days, but stress doesn't work that way at all. I had to teach myself to accept that this was going to be a journey. Before I could make positive changes, I needed to do the groundwork of understanding the sources of my stress. One of the biggest sources was my lack of self-care. Doing everything for everyone can take a toll on a person, especially when they are not also taking time to care for themselves. I don't mean that I was down and out and didn't take showers or groom myself. Actually, it was the opposite. I functioned well in society but was burned out inside. I needed to be intentional about caring for myself mentally, physically, and emotionally and I needed to do all of this prior to pouring into everyone else.

When I talked to my doctor, she suggested I view stress as a scale or a meter that spans from 0 to 10. The meter fluctuates often throughout each day. The goal is to maintain a stress level of 0 to 2. Levels 3-5 are manageable, and as the numbers increase, so does the severity. Some people have no issues managing their stress, and then there are many people who need to take time to do activities to reduce stress. For the latter group, not doing stress-reducing activities causes our stress levels to hover higher on the scale than we'd like. Continuously neglecting to reduce stress can lead to chronic stress, which leads to a host of problems.

Learning this caused me to switch my focus from relieving anxiety to relieving stress. This opened a new world for me because most of my research pointed to self-care activities. I discovered that if I wanted to reduce my stress, I needed to submerge myself into self-care. I decided to make a self-care calendar. I researched self-care activities. I scheduled time on my calendar for these activities. I watched videos, read books, and listened to podcasts. I did everything I could to learn as much about self-care and to practice self-care. I learned to meditate so I could focus on the present, not the past or the future. See, part of my issue was that I was, and still am, an overthinker. I also pay attention to details and overanalyze everything. I would sit and think about a situation and overthink that situation coming up with scenarios that would never happen. I would think myself into an unnecessarily stressful situation. Meditation was part of the answer to understanding that the present is what matters, the past has already happened, and no one knows what the future will bring. If the pandemic taught us nothing else, it taught us that. I learned and still need reminders to focus on what is in my control and to forget about, or at least don't try to control, what is not in my control.

I made my self-care plan non-negotiable and prioritized self-care first before anything else. To make this journey fun, I created a list of all the self-care activities I wanted to try. See the list in Chapter 8. If you somehow missed it, the list contains over 100 self-care activities. There is something for everyone. If I loved something, I did it multiple times. I also added my friends to the plan. I chose three friends and scheduled individual friend dates every six weeks. I figured six weeks was enough time to live life, do something wild, and have a story to tell at the next lunch or dinner. It was amazing.

To overcome stress, I also needed to stop doing some things. I needed to stop telling other people to take better care of themselves while I wasn't doing the same. I needed to stop neglecting myself and stop trying to pour from an empty cup, which sometimes looks like telling people "No" and not overcommitting or overextending. Now, I practice what I preach. All of this has allowed my stress meter to lower itself. It no longer hovers at 7 or 8. A few times, I think it went down to 0. Having three children doesn't allow it to stay at 0, or at least I haven't mastered that yet, but I am able to keep it down to a 3, which allows me more room to fill my cup and other people's cups, too. Again, it's a work in progress. It isn't easy, but it's worth it, and when I catch myself falling off track, I quickly jump back on and remind myself that my self-care journey is a marathon, not a sprint.

11:11 My Purpose

To continue to become a better version of myself, I began to live in my purpose. While this may sound creepy or strange to some, others will completely understand. Many of us go through life without knowing our purpose, while some people know it from childhood. I am not one who has known my purpose since childhood, but I always knew I wanted to help other people and be a light in the lives of others. That's really vague, right? I know. However, during the pandemic, I realized that my experiences and my purpose are aligned. The dots of my past started to connect, and I started seeing clear signs of what my purpose was and still is today. So, here's my story of how I found my purpose.

I started getting strong feelings that it was time to publish my self-care book. The feelings were equally as strong as the feelings prior, the ones that told me not to publish the book. The problem was that I had lost interest in publishing. Over the course of a year or so, I would toy around with the idea of finishing the book but writing a book is so much work that it's something you need to really want to do, or else it will not happen. Whenever I tried to write or edit what was previously written, I found myself wanting to do other things: wash the dishes, clean the house, go shopping, literally, anything besides write or edit. I knew the book could possibly help someone, but I am a private person, so I wasn't sure how to tell my story or how much of my story I should tell. I also wasn't sure how to tell my own story, but also turn the book into a personal development book for others. It felt like a task I was no longer interested in completing, so I continued to let the manuscript sit. Every so often, I would get another nudge, another sign to finish the book. The nudge would prompt me to attempt to try again, only to sit the book down again. But the final nudge came when I discovered 11:11.

I'd convinced myself that I could finish the book within a week if I focused one hundred percent of my time on it. A few days into editing, I became restless and wanted to listen to music. The internet in my house can be iffy at times. Sometimes, the service drops for a short period of time and then returns randomly. I am used to it, so when it happened earlier this year, for days, I didn't think anything of it. Most people cannot go days without internet service, so let me make that make sense. I don't watch T.V. often, and I can sit in silence for days at a time. When I realized the internet was down, I assumed it would be back up again soon, as usual, and I focused my attention back on writing the book in silence. This went on for a few days.

Finally, I said enough is enough, and I needed some sort of background noise. I have an old DVD player and a few old DVDs. I never use them, but without the internet, I could not get the T.V. or my music to work. I opted for the DVD player. When I went to plug in the DVD player, I realized how dirty the T.V. stand was, so I went to get a cloth and spray to clean the stand. While cleaning the T.V. stand, I noticed a pamphlet. The pamphlet was from Wildwood, New Jersey. I had just written about pamphlets, so it caught my eye. I looked at the date and it was from 2011. I was surprised because I had only been living in my house for two years and it was more than a decade since the pamphlet had been created. On top of the pamphlet, I found a flashcard, just one single flashcard with the number 11 on it. I laughed and said, "11:11, interesting." I didn't think too much of it at the time. I had heard of 11:11 but didn't know the full meaning. I had heard people say, "11:11, make a wish," but that was the extent of my 11:11 knowledge. I took a mental note to research the meaning of 11:11, and I threw the pamphlet and the flashcard in the trash. I turned the movie on and then went back to writing.

The next day, I needed a break from writing, so I went on social media to get a bit of a break. Someone I follow had just posted a picture of their hair, and she tagged the hairstylist. I clicked on the stylist's profile to see more of her work. When I clicked the profile, a gallery of pictures appeared. I scrolled and then clicked a random picture. The picture opened and showed an image of the stylist's tattoo. Her tattoo read, "11:11." I was intrigued by the reappearance of 11:11. I had not done any research yet, but this was confirmation that I needed to figure this out. I immediately went on YouTube to see if I could find videos about 11:11. The first video that appeared was a Chris Brown album titled 11:11 that had just been released less than two months prior. I was more interested than ever before. I started watching videos. While each video made different points, all of them had similarities. Based on the videos, 11:11 means you are in touch with the universe, you are in touch with God, and you are in touch with your spiritual purpose. It also means you are on the right track and on the mission you are supposed to be on. I learned that 11:11 is not the only set of numbers that have this meaning and that it could be 111, 222, 1010, and so on. Each set of numbers has a different meaning. I was mind-blown. At the time, the only mission I was on was to finish the book. I took it as a sign that I was on the right track and that, this time, I was actually supposed to finish and publish the book.

I was so excited about my new discovery that I went outside, searching for 11:11 everywhere. I went to the gas station and looked for the numbers on different pumps. I looked at buildings and billboards, hoping to see those numbers. Like most things, when you are looking for them, you don't see them. Later that day, I left to pick my daughter up from the hairdresser. Still stoked about my findings, I kept looking for 11:11. As I drove down the street, a car in front of me started reversing quickly. I had to slam on the brakes because they were coming toward me so fast. The person in the car was trying to park the car, so I sat there and waited until they finished parking. As they were backing into the parking space, I looked over to the left and noticed the addresses on the houses. The house directly to my left had a written sign that read, "One Eleven." I was floored. I could not believe my eyes. I picked up my phone and took a picture of the house. From that moment on, I knew my purpose was to finish rewriting my book and then share it with the world.

So many people are in the place I've been countless times before. If they aren't in the same place, they may be somewhere similar. So many people need to hear, read, and learn about preventing burnout, stress, and other health issues. People need to learn to take better care of themselves mentally, physically, and emotionally. I want to share the message of self-care with everyone who will listen. If I can help just one person, then I will know that my writing was not in vain, but I know this mission is much larger than that. I've learned that a large part of my self-care journey is about helping others. I am pouring into others because that is what I was born to do, but doing so in a way that takes care of myself first, so I am better equipped to take care of everyone else around me.

I am asking other people to pour into themselves first so that they can better care for the people around them. I am scheduling quarterly Self-care Assessment Meetings with myself, asking myself which ways I want to show up for myself unselfishly. I am making sure my cup stays full enough that I can pour into others, and I am thanking God for providing me with the vision, skills, and experience to be able to share my story in a way that can help others who may be in the same situation I was in. If you are that person or if you resonate with any of the people or stories mentioned in this book, know that you are not alone, and it's never too late to start or enhance your very own self-care journey. This is how I became a better version of myself, and if I can do it, so can you.

The end... for now.

Notes

Notes

Notes

Notes

Notes

Notes

Notes

Notes

LaToya D. Thomas was born and raised in Philadelphia, PA and continues to live in the Pennsylvania area. She has three children and a fur baby named Journey. LaToya graduated from Bellevue University with a Bachelor of Science degree in Behavioral Science. Prior to that, she received an associate degree in early childhood education, which was the start of her career working with children and families.

LaToya began publishing children's books in 2018. Her debut book, You Are Beautiful, Beautiful You Are, an Amazon Bestseller, was the first in the Self-Love and Encouragement series. The series sought to teach children to accept themselves and their differences, to love themselves and others, to understand that we are braver than we know, and lastly, that happiness is a choice.

When she isn't working or writing, LaToya enjoys reading nonfiction books, researching, swimming, and shopping. She loves traveling, and recently traveled to Africa to spend nearly a month in Kenya.

In the future, LaToya hopes to serve as an inspiration to others, both through her books and in everyday life. She plans to host much-needed workshops and share the message of the importance of self-care.

www.ingramcontent.com/pod-product-compliance
Lightning Source LLC
Chambersburg PA
CBHW071706120626
46550CB00001B/123